THE FIRST APARTMENT BOOK

4 R

THE FIRST APARTMENT

COOL DESIGN FOR SMALL SPACES

KYLE SCHUNEMAN

WITH HEATHER SUMMERVILLE

photographs by joe schmelzer

CLARKSON POTTER/PUBLISHERS
NEW YORK

Published in the United States by Clarkson Potter/Publishers, an imprint of the
Crown Publishing Group, a division of Random House, Inc., New York.
www.crownpublishing.com
www.clarksonpotter.com

CLARKSON POTTER is a trademark and POTTER with colophon is a registered
trademark of Random House, Inc.

Library of Congress Cataloging-in-Publication Data
Schuneman, Kyle.
    The first apartment book / Kyle Schuneman with Heather Summerville. —1st ed.
        p. cm.
    Includes index.
1. Apartment houses.   2. Interior decoration.   I. Summerville, Heather.   II. Title.
    NK2195.A6S38 2012
    747'.88314—dc23   2011043290

ISBN   978-0-307-95290-5
eISBN 978-0-307-95291-2

Printed in China

Book and cover design by Rae Ann Spitzenberger
Cover photography © Joe Schmelzer

10 9 8 7 6 5 4 3 2 1

First Edition

CONTENTS

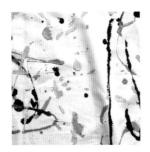

INTRODUCTION

I'VE ALWAYS LOVED THE SKY-IS-THE-LIMIT MENTALITY THAT COMES WITH MOVING IN TO A NEW APARTMENT.

So what if you can measure the whole space in arm-lengths, and the floor plan looks more like a half-finished game of dominoes? It's yours—and it's home.

Hours are whiled away daydreaming of the cool—occasionally off-the-wall—ways you're going to put your stamp on this tiny space. (Midnight-black walls? Most definitely.) Then reality bursts your design bubble. Those ugly cabinets you want to paint . . . turns out it's not allowed. The sofa you've had an eye on . . . it's not even close to being within your budget. Every creative outlet ends in a frustrating "no." And giving up to the humdrum view of four white walls seems inevitable.

Hey, I've been there—and everyone involved in the making of this book has too. It's a rite of passage, I'm afraid. But as I often say, every "no" is surrounded by a sea of "yeses." There is always a way to make your design vision come true—you just have to get a little more creative in how you go about it.

Consider this book your personal guide—it's everything I wish I knew when I was starting out. It's smart decorating. It's inspiration. It's how-tos. It's real stories about real people in real "starter" apartments. It's the book that gives you permission to stick your head in the clouds and dream big. Because, after all, that's what your first apartment is for.

WHAT YOU'LL FIND INSIDE

Each of the ten chapters in *The First Apartment Book* tackles a different style aesthetic and a different set of real-life design obstacles: The Art Lover in New York City who needed to turn her one-room studio into four functional spaces; The Collector in Los Angeles who stockpiles porcelain figurines and needed an organized means of displaying them; The Roommates in Boston who couldn't figure out how to combine their strikingly different tastes. These are real apartment makeovers, real budgets, and real scenarios based on the (often frustrating) living situations my friends and I have found ourselves in over the years—and inside these pages are all the helpful lessons I came away with. You'll find floor plans, cost breakdowns, and how-to projects in every chapter—and not just a checklist of what I did, but also the "why" behind it. And the sources for everything you see—right down to the paint color on the walls—can be found in our Resources section.

The First Apartment Book is meant to be easy, useful, and, more than anything else, fun. You can relate to our renters' situations, and like them, you will (I hope!) find humor in the small-space decorating predicaments they find themselves in—because laughter is the one surefire ingredient that can make a 500-square-foot apartment feel like your own mini-mansion.

CLOCKWISE FROM TOP LEFT:
Edgewater in Cleveland; Miracle Mile in LA; Cow Hollow in San Francisco; Inman Park in Atlanta; The Space Needle in Seattle; East Nashville; The "T" in Boston; West Village in New York City; Burnham Park Fountain in Chicago.

GETTING STARTED:
APARTMENT HUNTING 101
TEN TIPS YOU DON'T KNOW—BUT SHOULD

1

FORGET YOUR MANNERS. Open every closet, every cabinet door, and every kitchen drawer. Storage comes at a premium in small spaces; you need to know what you're starting with.

2

FLUSH THE TOILET—and while you're at it, turn on the shower. There is absolutely nothing you can do about bad plumbing once you've moved in. Low water pressure is an automatic red flag.

3

SHOW UP TO A RENTAL LISTING PREPARED. Good apartments don't last long. If you have a letter of recommendation and proof of good credit handy, you'll be miles ahead of your competition.

6

TAKE IN THE VIEW— AND NOT JUST THE SKYLINE. Do you see construction happening around the building? A metal shop? Train tracks? All of these things make noise, even if you don't hear a peep when you're in the apartment.

7

HOW MUCH IS MILK AT THE LOCAL CONVENIENCE STORE? Find the nearest grocery store, drugstore, and Laundromat—and check out the pricing. Paying more for the essentials will take a huge chunk out of your monthly budget.

4

DO A DRIVE-BY.
Most apartment
viewings happen
during the day, when
everyone is at work.
To get a more accurate
feel for the block and
the parking situation,
walk by after dark,
or use Google Maps
Street View to cyber-
stalk your potential
new neighborhood.

5

**BOOKMARK THIS
SITE:** BedbugRegistry.
com. Before you
even check out an
apartment, type
the address into
this registry. It will
tell you if there has
been an encounter
with bedbugs at this
address, and when.
(It's better to know,
right?)

8

**NEVER JUDGE AN
APARTMENT BY ITS
EXTERIOR**—judge it
by its hallways. Are they
clean? Is mail strewn
across the floor? Do
your neighbors junk-up
the space with personal
items? Neighbors
who don't respect the
common areas don't
make good neighbors.

9

**MAP OUT THE BIG
STUFF.** It's tricky to
envision spacing in
an empty apartment,
so check out the wall
situation. If every
wall has a window
or doorway, where
is your sofa or bed
going to fit?

10

**CALL SOMEONE WHO
CARES.** Make sure
you have cell phone
reception in every
room. If you wait until
moving day to discover
your phone only works
while hanging out the
bedroom window, well,
it's going to get lonely
fast.

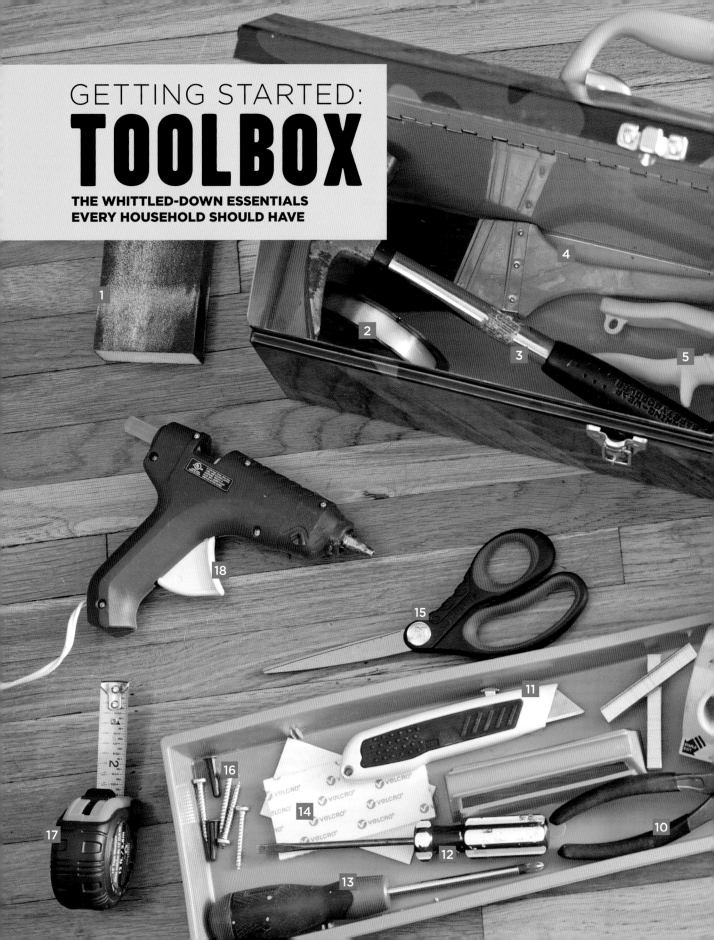

GETTING STARTED:
TOOLBOX

**THE WHITTLED-DOWN ESSENTIALS
EVERY HOUSEHOLD SHOULD HAVE**

THE TOOLS

1. Sanding block
2. Extra-strength fishing line
3. Rubber-handle hammer
4. 2- or 3-inch Purdy paint brush
5. Tin snips
6. 2-inch painter's tape
7. Stitch Witchery
8. Electric drill set with bits (12 volts or higher)
9. Basic staple gun with staples
10. Flat nose pliers
11. Utility knife with retractable blade
12. Flat head screwdriver
13. Phillips head screwdriver
14. Industrial-strength Velcro strips
15. Utility scissors
16. 1 pack, #10 screws and anchors
17. 12-foot tape measure (or longer)
18. High-temp glue gun with glue sticks

THE
ART
LOVER

THE ART LOVER

WHO: Janelle

JOB: Entry-level attorney

LIVES IN: Greenwich Village, NYC

MEASUREMENTS: 425 square feet

LIKE MANY A NEW YORK TRANSPLANT, JANELLE MOVED TO MANHATTAN WITH AN IMPRESSIVE DEGREE, A PIECEMEAL ASSORTMENT OF BELONGINGS, AND NO JOB OR APARTMENT.

After sixteen months of sofa-surfing, she landed an entry-level position with a law firm and found what's known in the New York rental market as a "pretty sweet deal": a tiny, rent-controlled studio in a fourth-floor walk-up in Greenwich Village. The one drawback: living in a space that could be measured in arm-lengths—two arm-lengths wide by five arm-lengths long.

A big part of finding your first apartment is coming to terms with what you can and cannot live without. Janelle forfeited convenience—those four flights of stairs are a doozy with groceries—for a trendy neighborhood that appealed to her first love: art. The six-unit row house she lives in was built in 1905 and once counted John Lennon and Yoko Ono as tenants. Everything from the strip of art galleries to the street artists on the corners became inspiration for Janelle's apartment. But the major design obstacle remained: how to make a one-room apartment (excluding the bathroom) function as four separate spaces—a place to sleep, a place to eat, a place to work, and a living room of sorts. It sounds like a tall order, but it was one I managed to pull together with some flea market scores, the few pieces of furniture she already owned, and artful flourishes inspired by some of the greats: Michelangelo, Damien Hirst, and Jackson Pollock.

YARN
FRAMES,
P. 27

NO-SEW
PILLOWS,
P. 33

POLLOCK
SLIPCOVER,
P. 19

A LIVING ROOM OF SORTS

TIP: Throw pillows are an easy way to add pops of color and texture to a room. But cheap, cool throw pillows are hard to come by—which is why it's often easier to make your own. Flip to page 33 for instructions on making the no-sew pillows you see on the sofa.

The loveseat was the biggest piece to make the 460-mile trek from Janelle's hometown of Cleveland (compliments of Mom and Dad, who drove it out when Janelle moved in). It converts into an extra bed for guests, and as luck would have it, it squeezed perfectly between the front door and the kitchen nook—and I do mean squeeze; there wasn't a quarter inch to spare. In terms of function, it was gold. But the loveseat originally belonged to Janelle's great aunt. It had been through a half-dozen moves already, and by the time it found its way to New York, it looked about a hundred years old. This is where you have to remember the mantra: "Don't judge a book by its cover." Or more appropriately in this case: "Don't judge a loveseat by its faded floral fabric." If the shape is there, the cover is always changeable.

The easy fix: buy a plain white slipcover (about $89) and call it a day. But when your whole apartment fits only five pieces of furniture, you want those five pieces to make a statement. So I used Jackson Pollock, one of Janelle's favorite artists, as inspiration for turning a basic slipcover into something far more fun. By straying from the obvious—turning the sofa into art and leaving the yarn frames (see page 27 for instructions on making these) empty on the walls above—I got the cool, downtown aesthetic I was after, and Janelle got a giant piece of functional art.

THE FLOOR PLAN

I start every design by mapping out a furniture plan, but this step is especially important for a small space. Janelle had two built-in architectural elements, a fireplace and a kitchen nook, that had to be accounted for, and she already owned a full-size bed and a loveseat. It was a complicated jigsaw puzzle that came down to measuring in inches. But I placed the biggest pieces first (a good rule of thumb) and came to terms with those elements that were just plain immobile, like the radiator. After that, it was simple to figure out what other furniture Janelle needed and where it would fit.

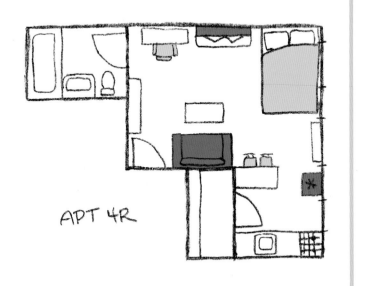

APT 4R

HOW-TO: POLLOCK SLIPCOVER

WHAT YOU NEED

- White canvas slipcover
- Drop cloth
- Fabric paint in 1-pint squirt bottles
- 1/2-inch-wide paintbrush
- 2-inch-wide paintbrush
- Spare bath towel or T-shirt
- Iron

STEP 1

Place your slipcovered sofa in the center of a drop cloth, and cover any walls within splashing distance. You're going to be slinging a lot of paint here.

STEP 2

Begin with your bigger strokes, which you get by making circles with your squirt bottle from a high distance—at least 4 feet from the slipcover. You can test your technique first on a spare bedsheet, or start on a side of the sofa that borders the wall.

STEP 3

Go over your original strokes with the 1/2-inch-wide paintbrush, making sure you follow the natural lines of the splatter. Lightly retracing your strokes is a must; otherwise, you end up with bumpy dried-paint splatters that can crack.

STEP 4

You can always add more paint, but it's impossible to erase what's already hit the canvas—so err on

the side of restraint. Once you're happy with the basic outline, take the 2-inch-wide paintbrush, wet it with water, and dip the tip of the brush in your paint. Then flick paint speckles over the remaining white space by tapping the brush handle against your palm from a distance of at least 2 feet above the slipcover.

STEP 5

Let the paint dry for about 24 hours. Then place your towel or T-shirt over a single section of the sofa at a time, and using medium heat, iron that section for 2 minutes, keeping the iron moving at all times. The heat sets your colors so they won't fade, making your masterpiece a permanent work of art.

A QUICK NOTE ON SLIPCOVERS

Make sure you're buying the correct slipcover for your sofa—and that the fabric has the right amount of structure and stretch to ensure a proper fit. Here are a few helpful shopping tips:

- If your sofa has attached back cushions, you need the two-piece slipcover.

- If the cushions come off, you need the three-piece style.

- And in general, avoid the one-piece styles, which end up looking like your sofa is wearing a sad muumuu.

"INSPIRATION IS ON EVERY STREET CORNER IN EVERY CITY. YOU'VE JUST GOT TO GET OUT THERE, EXPERIENCE IT, AND TAKE A LITTLE PIECE BACK HOME WITH YOU— WHETHER IT'S A PAINT COLOR, A PATTERN, OR SIMPLY THE RUSTY FINISH OF A LAMPPOST."

AN INSPIRED PALETTE

Janelle wanted her apartment to have a gallery-like feel. But in a city that kicks up as much grime as New York, white walls don't stay white for long. So I picked a more modern neutral, a warm slate gray, to use on the walls—which made the space feel pristine, but also lived-in. Then I introduced a palette of primary colors inspired by Janelle's new neighborhood: taxicab yellow, a blue to match a strand of rope from a flea market, and copper accents prompted by the street signs on her block.

A PLACE TO WORK

Janelle needed a small workspace. After getting the sofa and bed situated, the only area left for one was between the fireplace and the bathroom door. The wall was plenty wide for a desk, but the problem was the depth of the space. I needed something that was exactly as deep as the small nook created by the fireplace; otherwise, it would block the entrance to the bathroom, and no one wants to be bumping into furniture on the way to the loo after a night out in the Village.

I scoured every flea market and thrift store on the lower half of Manhattan before finding the perfect desk at a Salvation Army Store for $20 (and like a true New Yorker, I toted it twelve blocks back to the apartment in the rain). I also found a rather expensive-looking aluminum chair at the local Hell's Kitchen Flea Market for $40. The lesson here is that patience does pay off. I know it can be frustrating digging through these sorts of bargain-basement spots. But trust me, you will eventually find what you need, and the effort you put out now will make you love your space even more in the future.

TIP: Spread your accent colors around your space, instead of grouping them in one spot. It keeps the eye moving, and it gives the whole room a cohesive flow.

RIGHT: All the doors were in pretty bad shape, thanks to multiple layers of botched paint jobs. Covering them with a coat of semigloss black masked the rough edges.

OPPOSITE: Most flea market finds need a little love and care: new knobs, a good scrubbing, some paint. Investing a few more dollars in the small details will make all the difference.

NOT JUST BRICKS AND MORTAR

Original brick fixtures, like Janelle's nonworking fireplace, are common in many turn-of-the-last-century buildings. Most renters would pay a premium price to have that sort of classic detail. But the crumbling, brown-brick fireplace in Janelle's studio felt less charmingly old world and more out-of-date. It was the natural focal point of the room, and I wanted to keep it that way, but it needed to be streamlined. So I decided to paint it white, the only color the landlord would allow, and I covered the oak mantel with two coats of black semigloss paint. The end result: a completely modern fireplace more on a par with the rest of Janelle's apartment.

THE DO'S OF PAINTING BRICK

Do: Start by removing as much soot as possible from the brick with a wire brush—so the soot doesn't end up mixing with the paint.

Do: Buy masonry paint whether your fireplace is working or not. It's fireproof and costs the same per gallon as normal paint.

Do: Use a lamb's wool roller; it is thicker and can get paint down into those pesky brick crevices.

ART IS IN THE EYE OF THE BEHOLDER

TIP: An empty fireplace makes for great displays. Fill it with plants, coral, even logs the way we did here. Just be sure to use something big enough to make a visual impact. Anything too small will just disappear.

Once Janelle's fireplace underwent a twenty-first-century makeover, I wanted to go back and add those special little touches that make a space feel personal. I found these busts for $20 on a website called Plaster Craft. They were a nod to another of Janelle's art inspirations, Michelangelo. Left white, they felt a tad too kitschy. But spray-painted a semigloss taxicab yellow, they were the perfect, tongue-in-cheek nod to Renaissance art in modern-day New York. Then I framed a page from Janelle's grandfather's yearbook, which I discovered while going through a box she'd yet to unpack, and I added it to the mantel. Remember, art can come from anywhere; the arrows on the wall were actually part of the shipping materials in a box I received. One coat of semigloss black paint, and they became a striking wall treatment that was light enough to hang on brick. Some of the best decorations come from things you already own. So before you go out and spend a single dollar, dig through those boxes you've been hoarding and see what sorts of gems you can uncover.

HOW-TO: YARN FRAMES

WHAT YOU NEED

- An assortment of wooden picture frames of varying sizes
- 1 skein of medium-weight yarn in your color of choice*
- Light-duty staple gun with ¼-inch staples

STEP 1

Put a movie on, pour a glass of wine, and get cozy. These are supereasy—and supercute—but they take a while to finish.

STEP 2

Grab a frame and get started. Staple the loose end of your yarn to the top left corner on the backside of your frame—just to the right of where the two sides meet at an angle.

STEP 3

Loop the yarn around the frame twice, pulling it tight. You want it to be flush but not so strained that it could break. Staple the yarn against the backside of the frame again. This ensures that your yarn is secure and won't start unraveling.

STEP 4

Start wrapping! Working in a clockwise motion, loop the yarn a dozen or so times, and then scrunch it down toward the already wrapped end to make the effect more substantial. Do an extra layer around the corners, where yarn tends to slip. Don't worry about things being perfectly straight or the same thickness.

STEP 5

Once you've made it all the way around, staple one end of your yarn to the backside of the frame. Wrap twice, and staple again to keep the end from unraveling. Once fastened, cut the yarn, leaving about an inch extra after the staple to ensure against future slippage.

STEP 6

Staple every 3 inches along the backside of your frame, making sure to do an extra "security" staple at an angle on each corner. This will keep your yarn wrap in place no matter how many years it hangs on the wall.

Note: It takes about 30 minutes to complete an 8- by 8-inch frame.

*One skein is enough to cover 5 average-size frames—around 8 by 8 inches.

4

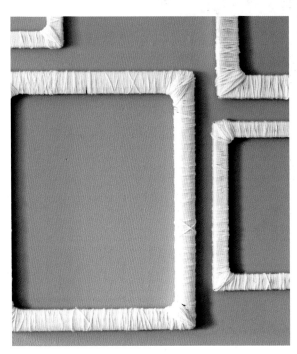

TIP: Removing cabinet doors is simple: just unscrew the hinges affixed to the main unit, and they come right off. Just don't lose any of the pieces; you'll need to reattach them when you move out—or risk losing a huge chunk of your security deposit.

A PLACE TO EAT

Janelle has never made anything more complicated than scrambled eggs and toast in her kitchen. Like most New Yorkers, dinner at home involves either take-out or delivery. But that didn't mean she was okay with her kitchen being an eyesore. As it was, the dirty white walls blended into the dirty white cabinetry and made for a wholly uninspiring space.

My first task was to get rid of the white. I started by covering the entire back wall in chalkboard paint. It's a guaranteed blast when friends come over, and like so many other places in Janelle's apartment, it became a spot for her to enjoy rotating art. Then I removed the front doors of the wall cabinets, backed the cabinets with a foiled wallpaper, and painted the entire unit the same slate gray as the walls in the rest of the space. Now the metallic backing really catches the light, so when the glassware was inside the cabinet, everything had a beautiful sparkle—making the whole unit look far fancier than it actually was.

OILCLOTH (NOT JUST FOR MEXICAN RESTAURANTS ANYMORE)

Janelle picked up a tall bar table at Pier One's Black Friday sale two weeks after moving in. The shape and height were perfect, acting as a small island separating the kitchen from her sleeping area, but the faux-wood top and forest green legs felt too woodsy for Janelle's gallery-like aesthetic. So I painted the legs of the table the same slate gray as the cabinets and the walls, and I covered the top with (in my opinion) a highly underappreciated fabric: oilcloth.

Oilcloth wipes clean and is dirt cheap. Sure, it comes in some crazy prints, but if you stick to the basics—like the stripes I used here—you really can't go wrong. It's sold by the yard at almost any fabric store, and it even has a few dedicated e-sellers on Etsy (Oilcloth Addict, for instance). One yard of oilcloth was enough to cover the top of Janelle's table. I simply lined up the stripes flush with the edges, folded the sides under, and securely stapled the fabric to the underside of the table with a staple gun.

The bar table separates the kitchen from the rest of the apartment, but I didn't want it to feel too closed off. Backless stools help keep the space nice and open.

SEEING STRIPES

Like so many of the other touches I added to Janelle's apartment, the black-and-white striped pattern of the oilcloth bar table was inspired by her new neighborhood. The buildings on her small street were dotted with classic black-and-white striped awnings. To bring a little more of that old-school vibe inside, I repeated the stripe in myriad ways around the rest of the apartment.

In the sleeping area, run-of-the-mill white wooden blinds we ordered from PaylessDecor.com were customized—at no extra charge—to include black banding (instead of plain-old white) on the front. Then in the bathroom, I went for a really bold effect and painted bigger stripes all the way around the room, giving the space a modern, French parlor feel. Repeating a graphic pattern, like these stripes, is a great way to visually break up a small space. Don't be afraid to use your imagination though; slight variations of the same pattern makes for a more unique finish.

HOW-TO: PAINTING STRIPES

WHAT YOU NEED

- Painter's tape
- Drop cloth
- Pencil
- Measuring tape
- Level
- Semigloss paint
- Paint roller
- Mod Podge Gloss All-in-One Clear Sealer (optional)

....

STEP 1

Prep the area for painting. Tape off the ceiling, floorboard, and any molding with painter's tape, and put down a drop cloth.

STEP 2

Starting in a corner by the shower or behind a door, mark off 6-inch* segments all the way around the room with your measuring tape and pencil. You'll need to eyeball where to put your last stripe, which may not be a perfect 6 inches from where you began.

STEP 3

Once your spacing is worked out, use your level and pencil to make dots every foot or so down the length of the wall at each of your 6-inch marks.

STEP 4

Line up the edge of your tape with the dots you just made, making sure the bulk of the tape is on top of the stripe that will be left white. Otherwise, your measurements will be off when you paint.

STEP 5

To ensure a nice, clean stripe you can—but don't have to—brush a single coat of Mod Podge along the seams of your painter's tape. It will keep paint from bleeding underneath your tape in places where the wall might not be perfectly even. Let dry for two hours.

STEP 6

Paint the appropriate stripe sections with two coats of semigloss paint, allowing an hour of drying time between coats. Remove your

TIP: Always use semigloss paint, not flat, in high-humidity rooms—it wipes down easily and won't leave water residue marks.

painter's tape, and clean up any accidental drip marks.

*In general, I like to do 6-inch stripes. They are big enough to have an impact but not so big that they make a room feel small.

HOW-TO:
NO-SEW
PILLOWS

HOW-TO: NO-SEW PILLOWS

WHAT YOU NEED

- Fabric
- Pillow insert
- Sharp scissors
- 1 roll of 1-inch Stitch Witchery regular tape
- Damp dishtowel or washcloth
- Iron
- ³/₈-inch grommet kit

....

STEP 1

Cut two fabric squares 3 inches larger than your pillow insert. For example, if your insert is 16 inches square, you want two 19-inch squares of fabric.

STEP 2

Lay one of your fabric squares on a flat surface, pattern side facing up. Cut four Stitch Witchery strips to match the length of the four sides of your fabric square.

STEP 3

Line up three of your Stitch Witchery strips along three of the outer edges of your fabric square. Lay your second fabric square on top, pattern side facing down, making sure all your edges are even.

STEP 4

Place your damp dishtowel or washcloth on a single section of the seam. Using the cloth as a guard, set the iron to medium heat, and press it down—don't slide it—for ten seconds. Repeat this process, completely tracing the border of the three sides that already have Stitch Witchery in place.

STEP 5

Once the Stitch Witchery is set and your seams are stuck together, turn your almost finished pillowcase inside out. The seams should be on the inside now. You're ready to insert your pillow.

STEP 6

To close up the last side, fold in 1-inch seams along the outer edge of both pieces of fabric—so you end up with what looks like a set of lips. Line up your last Stitch Witchery strip between the two folded-down seams, right along the edge; then iron it closed.

STEP 7

You can stop here. But if you want a little extra flair—or plan on having some heavy-duty pillow fights—you can insert grommets along the edges, which look cool and help keep the pillow together. Follow the directions on your grommet kit (they all work a little differently).

CHEAT SHEET:
THE ART LOVER

1
START WITH A FURNITURE PLAN. You have to know your measurements; otherwise, your "cheap find" that doesn't actually fit your apartment becomes an expensive problem.

2
LOAD UP ON INSPIRATION, but don't stray into theme-park territory. It's one thing to be inspired by the sights, sounds, and energy of a city like New York, but there are no Statue of Liberty posters and "I ♥ NYC" pillows in Janelle's apartment.

3
SPREAD YOUR ACCENT COLORS AROUND. It's the best—and easiest—way to tie all the elements in a space together.

4
THINK OUTSIDE THE BOX (the way we did with the Pollock slipcover). Your art doesn't always have to be on the walls.

5
PATIENCE IS A BARGAIN HUNTER'S VIRTUE. Don't rush into a purchase because you're tired of looking. You will eventually find the right piece—and all that effort will make you love it even more.

THE FREE SPIRIT

WHO: Megan

JOB: Tech strategist

LIVES IN: Cow Hollow, San Francisco

MEASUREMENTS: 750 square feet

UNTIL HER MOVE TO SAN FRANCISCO, MEGAN FELT MORE AT HOME ON A PLANE THAN IN ANY OF THE APARTMENTS WHERE SHE HAD BRIEFLY RESIDED.

The Chicago native lived in four places and four cities after leaving for college. She has traveled to thirty-five countries, and if she has her way, she will visit thirty-five more. But with a new job in a new city, the restless traveler was thinking of staying put for a while—or at least establishing a home base.

Megan arrived in the Bay Area fresh from a year in Hong Kong with two days to find an apartment. Thankfully, her search was limited to a very specific area: The No. 1 Muni Bus line, which stopped near her office. She found this ground-floor flat in SF's Cow Hollow neighborhood just in the nick of time. The 1930s Victorian building came with lots of built-in details—wainscoting and a nonworking fireplace, for instance—and even more wear-and-tear: the floors weren't exactly level, and the bathroom was separated into two washrooms. It was available immediately though, so she snapped it up.

Megan had whittled down her belongings to an impressive assortment of global keepsakes—and nothing in the way of furniture. Her parents were generous enough to ship out her old bedroom set. Otherwise, I was starting from scratch with a $1,000 budget to cover everything from bath towels to a sofa. Major penny-pinching went into creating this bright, happy apartment, which finally convinced Megan to hang up her well-worn backpack (at least for the time being).

PIECE BY PIECE

TIP: Side table not in the budget? Try a stack of books instead. Just make sure they're roughly the same size with plenty of hard covers thrown in to increase stability.

Buying your first "real" piece of furniture is a rite of passage, sort of like a step into adulthood—one that Megan had yet to experience until setting eyes on this vintage leather chair. We weren't planning to have extra seating in the living room because, quite frankly, it wasn't in the budget. But while perusing thrift stores and the clearance aisles of every boutique within walking distance, Megan spotted this midcentury modern chair for $150—and, well, it was love at first sight.

As important as it is to stick to your budget, it's equally important to allow these moments of treating yourself. Otherwise, decorating becomes a series of denied wishes. (Talk about bursting the excitement bubble.) This doesn't mean you should blow half your budget on one item, but making wise concessions along the way will keep the process fun.

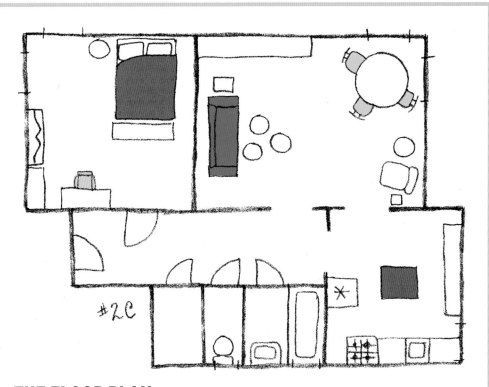

#2C

THE FLOOR PLAN

Megan's apartment is a series of chopped-up rooms off one long hallway. As was typical of buildings from this era, each room had its own door, and the kitchen actually had two—one leading in from the hall and one leading out to the living room. This was originally done to control the temperature of a room by closing it off. But since that's no longer an issue, the doors were just eating up a whole lot of space. In an attempt to visually open up the apartment, I removed the living room door and both kitchen doors, and I stored them in the building's basement. This created a natural flow through the public spaces, while still giving the bedroom and bathroom the privacy they needed.

RING OF CORAL

The living room was floor-to-ceiling white when I arrived—built-in woodwork, molding, coved ceiling, and all. But here's the downfall of an all-white room: it takes on whatever mood the natural light dictates. So in sunny LA, it would feel inviting. In San Francisco, however, where the fog rolls in like clockwork everyday at 4 p.m., four white walls can get a bit gloomy. Megan was used to the streamlined design aesthetic of Hong Kong, where strategic pops of color are freely mixed with streamlined décor and lots of natural light. I wanted to give her some semblance of that vibe here, so on our first shopping trip, I bought a bolt of discounted coral fabric in a heavy cotton-linen blend—and used it as the jumping off point for the color palette of the whole room.

My initial idea was to use it as backing for the built-in bookshelves, since we couldn't paint them. But it ended up coming in handy for so much more, like Roman blinds and seat cushions. It even inspired the paint color I used along the top of the wall. By keeping all the warm notes in this cheery hue, I could introduce a few cool tones, like the ice blue sofa and navy rug. Nothing was too matchy-matchy, which gave the room depth—and made all the architectural elements much more pronounced.

NICE STEMS

Hanging out, eating, and party hosting are all done in the confines of the living room—which is a whole lot of action for a 14- by 12-foot space. This also meant the biggest pieces of furniture—the sofa and the dining table—had to fit within the same four walls. The trick to keeping the space from feeling too cramped: long, lean legs. Everything we purchased—the sofa, the nesting tables, and the dining chairs and table—sat on thin, delicate legs. This removed the weight from the floor and dispersed it at different vertical levels throughout the room. So visually, it felt open and spacious.

Playing opposite ends of the color wheel off each other, like we did with the vibrant coral and cool blue notes here, is a great way to create harmony in a room—while still keeping things interesting.

HOW-TO: FABRIC-BACKED BOOKCASE

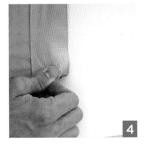

WHAT YOU NEED

- Measuring tape
- 4, 36- by 30-inch pieces of foam core board*
- Pencil
- Level
- X-ACTO knife
- Fabric
- Scissors
- Duct tape

STEP 1

Measure the width and height of the wall between each shelf. (You'll get the most precise dimensions if you measure the height in the center of the shelf and at both corners.)

STEP 2

Trace your measurements onto your foam core boards with a straightedge, double-checking that your top and bottom lines are level. Then carefully cut out each piece with your X-ACTO knife.

STEP 3

Dry test the fit. Slide each of your foam core pieces into its designated space. With old apartments, shelves can bow over time, so you may need to shave down certain areas for a proper fit. Make sure the foam core is snug enough to stay put without any help.

STEP 4

Cut pieces of fabric to fit each of your foam core backs, leaving an extra 2-inch border all the way around. Wrap each foam core piece with fabric the way you would a gift. Then secure the fabric edges to the back of your foam core piece with duct tape.

STEP 5

Slide your fabric-covered foam core pieces back into their designated shelf spaces—this time for good.

*Buy foam core board wider than the space you plan to cover. Putting two pieces together will create a visible break under your fabric.

DRAMATIC DRAPERY

TIP: Re-covering furniture with a thicker material—like our coral linen-cotton blend—means you can get away with placing the new fabric directly over the old, no seat cushion removal necessary. Simply cut it to fit, and attach it with a staple gun.

With its side-by-side, floor-to-ceiling windows, this corner of the living room is undeniably romantic, like an old New Orleans hotel. Until, that is, you take a glimpse out the window and realize you're at street level. While you're sitting at the table enjoying the morning sun and your breakfast, everyone who strolls by on the way to the bus can envy your bowl of Cheerios and cup of coffee. Needless to say, window treatments were a necessity, but figuring out something that balanced natural light with privacy was tricky.

I used a set of extra-long patchwork print curtains I found in a clearance bin to frame the windows; then I added a bit of structure by turning Megan's run-of-the-mill plastic blinds into expensive-looking Roman shades with my bolt of coral fabric (see page 49 for instructions on making your own Roman shades). The result was a shot of color offset by a barrage of pattern, which gave the space an old-world bohemian vibe—and still let in plenty of sunlight even with the Roman shades pulled down.

AIR GARDEN

The San Francisco flower markets are the best in the country—and Megan has always had a green thumb. But thanks to a grueling work schedule and non-existent outdoor space, having a garden was out of the question. Even house plants were too much of a commitment. I wanted her to have the option of indulging in the city's rampantly available fresh flowers when possible, though, so I constructed a pseudo-chandelier above the dining room table with glass bubble vases I got from CB2 and fishing line. When empty, they caught the sunlight and almost looked like light bulbs. When filled with flowers, they were simply stunning. In either case, they helped ground the bistro dining table, so it had a sense of permanency. Plus, the chandelier saved Megan from ever having to waste precious tabletop space on a centerpiece.

These vintage chairs are Danish modern, but the new metal table feels very industrial. The mix is definitely unexpected, but it works because in both cases the shapes are streamlined.

ROMAN SHADES

2

3

4

5

6

7

HOW-TO: ROMAN SHADES

WHAT YOU NEED

- Plastic blinds*
- Scissors
- Fabric**
- Fabric glue

STEP 1

Unclip your plastic blinds, pull them out to their maximum length, and lay them on the ground.

STEP 2

Now we're going to create the skeleton that will hold your fabric in place. Leave every tenth blind intact, but cut and remove the rest of the blinds from the fixture using your scissors. You'll need to cut along both sides of the pulley system that controls the blinds in order to get each blind out—just be sure not to cut the actual string.

STEP 3

Spread your fabric on the floor, and place your blinds on top. (They should still be pulled out to their maximum length.) Cut your fabric to fit your blinds with an extra 2-inch border all the way around.

STEP 4

Take your fabric glue, and make pinky-nail-sized dots every inch or so across the entire length of your top blind. Rotate the blind by hand, and adhere the glue side to the fabric. Work your way down, repeating this step at every blind.

STEP 5

Wrap the extra 2 inches of fabric over the two long sides of your remaining blinds. This should create a clean edge down the entire length. Once you've double-checked the straightness, glue the folded-over fabric to the edges of each blind, one at a time.

STEP 6

You can't wrap the fabric around the top or bottom of your blinds—it will keep them from working properly. Instead, fold the fabric so that the fold lines up with the top edge on top, and the bottom edge down below. Glue along the fold and stick it directly to the front side of the blind, making sure you have a clean, defined edge.

STEP 7

Let your blinds dry completely, about one hour. Then clip the top portion back into place.

*Keep in mind that if you convert the blinds provided by your landlord to Roman shades, you'll need to replace them when you move out.

**Sturdier fabrics work best for this. Avoid anything too sheer that will allow your glue dots to show through—even though they dry clear.

IN THE KITCHEN

More often than not, you'll find Megan mixing up some delicious new treat in the kitchen. She picked up baking as a hobby a few years back (even though her presence near an oven was once considered a fire hazard). But her kitchen, like the living room, was a sterile, white-on-white-on-more-white space—except for the butcher block island her boyfriend had made from a natural light-colored wood. She really loved all the charming old-timey details in the room, like the built-in cabinets and molding (even though they came with a stove that predated her existence). There was even a cutting board that slid out from above one of the drawers.

I wanted to give her a bright, happy space that highlighted the little things that made the room great—while drawing your eye away from the not-so-great details. So I repeated the same Roman shade treatment from the living room in the corner window. Then I used two different hues of a retro lavender-gray paint—based on the fabric—to outline specific points in the room. The distinct, boxed-out lines gave the whole kitchen a warm, crisp atmosphere—one you'd expect to smell like freshly baked cookies.

VIEW FROM THE TOP

One of Megan's favorite neighborhood hangouts used strategically placed mirrors to reflect the top-shelf offerings behind the bar. She really loved the effect, so we repeated it in her own kitchen. Instead of liquor bottles, however, I laid out her coaster collection, accumulated from her many travels. This type of mirror treatment is simple to rig up:

- Buy a cheap mirror.
- Angle it above your shelf.
- Secure the mirror with nails.

It's a cheap, easy way to make small-scale collections much more impactful.

TIP: Older drawer handles were often made in a length that's not sold anymore. When it comes time to replace them, use two single knobs in place of one long handle—they work just as well.

OPPOSITE: Leaving dishes and glassware out in the open has a great low-key vibe. But to keep things feeling clean and crisp it's best to display them against a white background.

THE MODERN ROMANTIC

What's now Megan's bedroom was originally the living room—hence the existence of a fireplace and the nonexistence of a closet. As this space was the smaller of the two rooms, it made sense to switch them. But the lack of available uninterrupted wall area meant the bed could fit in only one place—the wall opposite the door—leaving no room for Megan's low dresser. I had to push the dresser against the foot of the bed in order to keep it in the room. But putting something so large at the foot of the bed meant that Megan's lack of a headboard was even more pronounced. To divert attention back where it belonged, something dramatic was needed at the top of the bed.

The rest of Megan's apartment had a sophisticated subtleness to it. Since the bedroom sat off by itself, we could get away with trying something bolder. So I found this extra-high tufted headboard on Amazon.com for about $200—my last major purchase—and planned to place it against a Moroccan-inspired temporary wallpaper (see page 55 for application instructions). Megan's timid response to the adventurous pairing was, "Let's see what it looks like." Sometimes going a little outside your comfort zone is the only way to make the big statement you're after. Megan would never have gone for this wallpaper on its own, but using it as a background for lots of crisp, white details—the headboard, the comforter, the lamp shade, the dresser—made everything pop, while keeping the focus of the room off the dresser and on this amazing new wall treatment.

TIP: Whenever possible, you should make your bed accessible from both sides— even if only by a foot, the way we did here. It automatically feels more grown up and sophisticated.

>> SECRET SOURCE

Tempaper by **Tempaper Designs** is brilliant. It goes on and pulls off just like a wall decal. Plus, there is an ever-growing selection of patterns to pick from at TempaperDesigns.com.

> ❝ **SOMETIMES GOING A LITTLE OUTSIDE** YOUR COMFORT ZONE IS THE ONLY WAY TO MAKE THE BIG STATEMENT YOU'RE AFTER.❞

Even though we were using a dresser and headboard to bookend her bed, it feels like one complete unit because the headboard, comforter, and dresser are all white.

WALL
PAPER

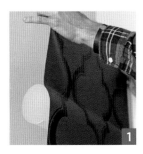

HOW-TO: TEMPAPER WALLPAPER

WHAT YOU NEED
- Tempaper
- Level
- Ruler
- X-ACTO knife

STEP 1
Peel the backing off the first 12 inches of your Tempaper. Line up the sticky portion in the top corner of the wall you want to cover—using the molding or ceiling as a guide.

STEP 2
Smooth the sticky portion onto the wall with the palm of your hand. Start at the top and smooth down—not side-to-side, which creates air bubbles.

STEP 3
Once this first portion is attached, check that it is actually level. Sometimes walls can bow, especially in older apartments. To keep your pattern straight, it's more important that the Tempaper is level rather than lined up perfectly with the ceiling.

STEP 4
After making any necessary leveling adjustments, continue attaching your Tempaper to the wall. Peel off 12-inch segments of backing at a time, and smooth your way down. You can keep using your palm, or you can use a ruler, which I find speeds things up and causes fewer air bubbles.

STEP 5
Once you reach the bottom—and your Tempaper is firmly and smoothly attached—trim any excess paper with an X-ACTO knife.

STEP 6
Using the pattern on your first sheet of Tempaper as a guide, line up your next piece—and start all over again. (Checking that it's level won't be necessary because, as long as your pattern is matching up, the Tempaper should remain level all the way across the wall.)

SOUVENIR SHOP

Megan coined the phrase "struggling minimalist" to describe her love of simple, clean-lined décor contrasted with a habit of accumulating lots of little things (jewelry, photographs, books, and keepsakes from her travels). The collection is always growing—and the items she likes to display is always changing. So I wanted to give her an informal spot where she could switch things out at will.

When I first arrived, she was using the fireplace mantel as a pseudo-bookshelf, but it was the perfect place to make impromptu arrangements. So I gave the books a new home by stacking them (paper side facing out) in the nonworking fireplace. Then I added her photos, stacked journals, and even an unframed glass mirror to the mantel instead. She could simply lean whatever she wanted against the back wall, without ever needing a hammer or nail—meaning absolutely nothing was permanent. The textured pages, combined with the white brick and geometric wallpaper, made the once unnoticeable area a focal point of the room.

>> SECRET SOURCE
The Italian brand **Mondial Lus** has been making sleek, colorful desk accessories since the 1930s. They have an entire selection of thumbtacks that come in the coolest/oddest colors, like coffee and dandelion. Visit sweetbellausa.com to see the selection.

FRAMELESS FRAMEWORK

There was a small work station in the corner of Megan's room. It was used for taking care of personal things more than actual work, which is why Megan found a spot for it—and promptly ignored it afterward. But the sparse setting and cold materials made the whole area feel unfinished. All the space needed was something on the wall to ground it, so I found an oil painting from China that Megan's brother had given her. It didn't have a frame, and there was no money left in the budget for one. So we simply lined its border with flat thumbtacks—never actually inserting the tack in the print but instead sticking the posts in the wall and using them as a sort of guide. Thumbtacks come in so many colors these days that you can find a shade that disappears into whatever you're hanging. Never let the lack of a frame deter you; unframed artwork, though much more relaxed in feeling, is far better than a completely bare wall.

The best displays are built from mementos, rather than expensive tchotchkes. Play around with different heights and textures, and no matter what you're showcasing, it will feel special and thoughtful.

CHEAT SHEET:
THE FREE SPIRIT

1
TAKE ADVANTAGE OF COLOR. Use it to highlight crisp white details, like furniture or architectural elements.

2
WHEN CARVING OUT A DINING AREA in a larger room, hang something above the table to ground it—like a homemade sculpture or chandelier.

3
LAYERED WINDOW TREATMENTS ALWAYS LOOK RICH and expensive—no matter how little you actually spend on them.

4
WALLPAPER ISN'T JUST FOR HOMEOWNERS ANYMORE. Thanks to the invention of Tempaper, everyone can enjoy the luxury of a statement wall in his or her apartment.

5
DON'T FORGET ABOUT VERTICAL SPACE. Furniture with long, lean legs will keep a room from feeling heavy and cluttered.

THE

PREPPY

THE PREPPY

WHO: Holt

JOB: Business manager for a local organic restaurant

LIVES IN: Edgewater, Cleveland

MEASUREMENTS: 701 square feet

AN OHIOAN AT HEART, HOLT MOVED BACK TO HIS HOME STATE AFTER FOUR YEARS AT AN IVY LEAGUE UNIVERSITY ON THE EAST COAST.

He left school with a top-notch degree, which helped him land a job as the business manager for an award-winning, farm-to-table restaurant in Cleveland—and a mountain of student loans. Like most grads, Holt had some harsh give-and-take realities to face. His dream job had a less-than-dreamy starting salary and a work schedule that included multiple evening shifts every week. Plus, the only apartments within his price range weren't located anywhere near the restaurant.

Holt finally found a one-bedroom apartment in an English Tudor–style building—which reminded him of his university dormitory, climbing ivy and all—on the outskirts of the up-and-coming Edgewater neighborhood. The building dated back to the 1920s and featured original woodwork, swirling ornamental moldings, and rooftop pillars marked with classic stone gargoyles. Holt loved the character of the ramshackle outside details, even if it meant the inside was a tad run-down.

My focus, thankfully, was precise: figure out how to make Holt's penchant for plaid and argyle feel fresh—not like one of his former professors' studies. By avoiding a traditional color scheme—reds, blacks, deep greens—and wielding a palette of sea blue, mossy green, slate gray, and brown instead, Holt's favorite prints ventured far outside their classic roots. Throw in stripes, pops of bright colors, and an eclectic range of inspirations, and Holt's apartment—though preppy in theory—became a successful lesson in mixing bold décor.

PATTERN PLAY

TIP: When shopping for furniture, don't avoid your favorite stores out of fear of sticker shock. Almost every boutique has a clearance section where you can score majorly discounted floor samples—which is how I came to buy Holt's $2,400 designer sofa for $600.

Layering patterns is the easiest way to add depth to a room. But it's also a very scary undertaking. The truth is, you can and should layer bold prints—and it's far easier than you think. Here, we had a palette of happy blues and earthy browns, but we were missing the one thing that would bring everything together: an area rug. Now if I'd stuck with a solid rug, the entire room would have fallen flat. The reason this plaid rug works so well, apart from blending with the existing color scheme, is that its most dominant lines flow in the same direction as the stripes on the sofa and Roman shades (see page 68 for instructions on making these ribbon-trimmed shades). So in short: layer on the patterns—just mind the color scheme and direction of your prints.

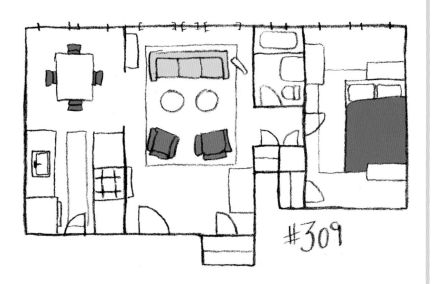

THE FLOOR PLAN

Holt's apartment was segmented into three distinct areas: the kitchen/dining room, the living room, and the bedroom/bathroom. Furniture placement wasn't going to be the tricky part—since Holt owned very little. Instead, I was more concerned with dividing the various preppy accents among the rooms. His collection ranged from equestrian décor to an überbright argyle print. Designating certain spaces for certain vibes was the only way to keep the apartment from venturing too far into clownish country club territory. So I staked out the kitchen/dining room as the "boys' night" arena, the living room as the more traditional setting, and the bedroom/bathroom as the place to be a little bold.

THE HAPPY BLUES

Holt wanted to transport some of the old-school collegiate charm he left on the East Coast to his new apartment in the Midwest. But I didn't want that to translate into a series of dark and gloomy rooms, so I focused on using lighter colors inspired by items he already owned. The blue I chose for the living room walls, for instance, matched the shade of the ocean on one of his globes, and the striped ribbon used on the blinds coordinated with a set of vintage bocce balls.

GLOBAL SUMMIT

I consider most radiators to be space-eating monstrosities, but this one actually came in handy (in addition to its obvious purpose of providing heat). It had an intricate, art deco–looking cover that only needed a fresh coat of semigloss white paint to feel new again. With the addition of two floating white shelves from Amazon.com, I was able to make something that felt like a built-in wall unit. I used the extra shelves to showcase part of Holt's impressive antique globe collection, a hobby he started back in the eighth grade.

HOW-TO: RIBBON-TRIMMED SHADES

WHAT YOU NEED

- Roman shades*
- Craft-quality ribbon (1 to 2 inches in width)**
- Measuring tape
- Crafter's hot-glue gun
- Glue sticks (on average, about 3 sticks per blind)
- Fabric scissors

STEP 1
First, we'll determine how much ribbon you need. Lay your Roman shade flat on the ground, open it completely, and measure the length. Add 4 inches to that measurement, and multiply by 2 (since you'll need a strip of ribbon for each side). Cut your ribbon to this length.

STEP 2
Decide how far from the edge of the shade you want your ribbon to be placed—between 2 and 4 inches works best. Measure that distance from the outside of your shade on both sides, making discrete tick marks down the entire length. Then line up the outside edge of your ribbon with these marks, leaving an extra 2 inches of length at the top and bottom of your shade.

STEP 3
Start gluing on low heat. Place small dots—about the size of a men's dress shirt button—every 2 inches or so along the center of the back side of your ribbon. Hot glue dries quickly, so make two or three dots and then flatten that section to the shade by sliding the palm of your hand down the entire length. (Be careful, it's hot!)

STEP 4
Take the extra 2 inches of ribbon from the top and bottom of your shade and fold them over the backside, making sure to get a nice, tight edge. Then adhere the ends to the backside with a few dots of glue—and you're done! Let dry for fifteen minutes before rehanging.

*This project only works on Roman shades. It would render horizontal blinds completely useless.

**When selecting your ribbon, avoid velvets, silks, and other fragile fabrics that won't stand up to hot glue.

DRESSING THE DRESSER

Holt found this small chest of drawers hidden underneath a pile of dusty boxes in his parents' basement. Functionally, it was just what he needed for his entry-way. Aesthetically though, it was a tad too prim and proper. So I decided to use a little decorative paper to tone down the stiffness of this turn-of-the-last-century, English dresser. I faced all the drawers with a subtle, grid-like plaid paper that added tons of personality without totally working against the piece's natural lines. You can do this on just about any surface.

HOW-TO: PLAID DRESSER

WHAT YOU NEED

- Measuring tape
- Decorative paper*
- Scissors
- 32-ounce bottle of Mod Podge Matte
- 2-inch-wide paintbrush
- X-ACTO knife

....

STEP 1

Pull the drawers out of the dresser, and remove all knobs and hardware; then give the drawer fronts a good cleaning.

STEP 2

Measure the face of each drawer. Then cut pieces of decorative paper to fit, leaving a 2-inch border of extra paper around the actual measurement of the drawer. If your paper isn't quite long enough to cover the entire drawer front, piece together two separate sheets. Just be sure to match up the prints carefully.

STEP 3

Apply a liberal coat of Mod Podge to the front of your drawer with a 2-inch brush. You want the drawer to be thickly covered, but not gloppy or runny. I recommend doing short strokes in the same direction to get the best effect.

STEP 4

Apply a slightly thinner coat of Mod Podge to the back of your decorative paper, being extra careful not to tear the paper once it's wet. Again, short strokes in one direction work best.

STEP 5

Press the back side of your decorative paper to the front side of your drawer, basically sticking both Mod Podge–covered surfaces together. Center the paper as best you can, with the 2-inch border of extra paper framing the drawer. Don't rush! You have a few minutes before the Mod Podge becomes tacky.

STEP 6

Once the paper is in the correct place, make sure there are no bubbles or folds. If you see one, gently work it out with your fingers. Then firmly smooth the paper over the front of the drawer with the side of your hand.

STEP 7

Fold the 2-inch border of excess paper over the lip of the drawer, making sure you have a nice, clean edge; then fold it again into the inside of the drawer. This three-sided effect deters fraying caused by constant opening and closing.

STEP 8

Apply another coat of Mod Podge over the top of the paper, using the same brush technique. It dries clear and will work as a sealant, so be sure to really go over the paper's edges. Apply at least two coats, allowing twenty-five minutes of drying time between each.

STEP 9

Reattach any hardware you removed before the Mod Podge is fully dry. For knobs, simply find the screw holes with your finger, poke through with the tip of an X-ACTO knife, and carefully twist the screws in. Any other details, like the keyholes on this dresser, will have to be traced with your X-ACTO knife. Let dry for about an hour before sliding the drawers back into the dresser.

*You can find decorative paper sold in individual sheets—not rolls—at most craft stores. The key is picking one that is thicker than tissue paper but not quite as heavy as card stock. Think nice gift-wrapping paper.

STOP, DROP, AND ORGANIZE

I've never met a person who didn't need to come to terms with some aspect of how he or she lives. I've dealt with wet towel droppers, clothes-in-the-corner culprits, dirty dish hoarders—the list goes on and on. Holt is your typical entryway stripper. (It's not nearly as scandalous as it sounds.) Within minutes of walking in the door, he takes off his tie and belt, empties his pockets, and tosses everything into the built-in shelves next to his front door. When I got to his apartment, there were ties and belts stacked six-deep on the doorknobs. It's the small things that make a space feel cluttered, though. Holt needed to accept the fact that it was okay to keep these things in the entryway—as long as he had a place for them. Be honest with how you live, and it becomes so much easier to keep your life organized.

TO THE MARKET I GO

Holt needed a few items to make his entryway function as a drop zone. I spent Sunday trolling the local flea market for ideas and unearthed some small bowls for change, a vintage tie rack, a plaid magnet board for bills, and a set of lamps for the entryway table. I scored the whole lot for only $50.

The trick to making a shopping trip like this successful is setting out with an idea of the problem you need to fix but not necessarily the exact item you need to fix it. For instance, I could have spent all day sifting through tables for the perfect mail sorter and never found one—which would have been a total waste of time. Because I was willing to be a little creative, I found the plaid magnet board instead, which worked perfectly as a place for Holt to keep his bills.

DINING IN

When you host a social gathering it's inevitable that everyone ends up in the kitchen. Instead of fighting this fact, Holt embraced it by moving his monthly poker night with the boys to his dining room table, instead of the living room. There was just one problem: the space felt like a frat house with a beaten-up table surrounded by mismatched chairs and nothing on the walls. And what's more, this tattered hodge-podge sat right next to his pristinely renovated kitchen. It turned out that the actual table wasn't in bad shape. After nearly a decade in his parents' crawlspace, the joints were perfectly fine. But there were enough tiny scratches in the wood to give someone a splinter, so I decided it made the most sense to paint it. Two coats of semigloss white later, the table felt much more modern and really flowed with the rest of the kitchen.

Holt's ramshackle seating selection still left much to be desired—in some cases a fully functioning chair bottom. I'm not normally one to toss something out, but considering the state of these chairs, it was easier to call it quits and start from scratch. So I found these very cheap, very basic blue chairs at Target, which were $65 for a set of two. I felt they needed a little something though, so I added racing stripes with the leftover semigloss paint from the table. Remember, customizing isn't just for old or expensive pieces of furniture. There's always the possibility of making something brand new feel special and unique.

TIP: White walls can dwarf artwork. If whatever you're hanging isn't big enough to make an impact, paint a larger "frame" behind it, as I did here with the shot of blueberries. It creates a much more noticeable, gallery-like effect.

» SECRET SOURCE

Canvas on Demand (canvasondemand. com) is my go-to source for turning personal photos into art. The quality is always spot-on—plus, they're fast and affordable. They made this triptych of blueberry images for me in less than a week.

Think about how you use your electronics. Holt spends most of his free time cooking, so we put the TV in the kitchen. Now he can watch Food Network while making dinner.

The Great Themes   LIFE LIBRARY OF PHOTOGRAPHY

Special Problems   LIFE LIBRARY OF PHOTOGRAPHY

Photographing Nature   LIFE LIBRARY OF PHOTOGRAPHY

The Print   LIFE LIBRARY OF PHOTOGRAPHY

Great Photographers   LIFE LIBRARY OF PHOTOGRAPHY

The Art of Photography   LIFE LIBRARY OF PHOTOGRAPHY

Frontiers of Photography   LIFE LIBRARY OF PHOTOGRAPHY

Caring for Photographs / Display Storage Restoration   LIFE LIBRARY OF PHOTOGRAPHY

Photographing Children   LIFE LIBRARY OF PHOTOGRAPHY

Color   LIFE LIBRARY OF PHOTOGRAPHY

The Camera   LIFE LIBRARY OF PHOTOGRAPHY

PHOTOGRAPHY YEAR / 1978 EDITION

Light and Film   LIFE LIBRARY OF PHOTOGRAPHY

The Studio   LIFE LIBRARY OF PHOTOGRAPHY

PHOTOGRAPHY YEAR / 1979 EDITION

Photography As a Tool   LIFE LIBRARY OF PHOTOGRAPHY

PHOTOGRAPHY YEAR / 1977 EDITION

Travel Photography   LIFE LIBRARY OF PHOTOGRAPHY

Photojournalism   LIFE LIBRARY OF PHOTOGRAPHY

FAIRVIEW
H.S.

ARGYLE INSPIRATIONS AND PATTERNED DREAMS

Holt's tiny bathroom was your typical, functional, white-tiled washroom—no fussy flourishes, just the basics. The truth is, the white-tiled walls and old-fashioned fixtures worked just fine. Considering Holt's budget, I decided to leave well enough alone and spend what was left of the makeover allowance on something a little more necessary. So I found this argyle shower curtain in a retro mossy green and gray color palette, stocked up on some striped green towels, and considered the bathroom finished.

Little did I know then that the shower curtain would become the inspiration for the bedroom as well. I picked argyle because as far as prints go, it makes a complete statement all on its own. Plus, I took one look in Holt's sock drawer and knew he was a fan. The two small rooms are broken off into their own section of the apartment, so giving them one cohesive palette made the pair feel more like a joint bedroom/bathroom suite. Holt loved the old-school, *Caddyshack* appeal of the argyle so much that I decided to mimic it in the bedroom in a major way—so I painted an entire wall in an argyle pattern (see pages 80–81 for instructions on painting your own argyle wall). In theory, it may seem a tad intimidating, but the segmented effect of the argyle actually gave the tight, narrow bedroom the illusion of greater depth.

FLIP FOR IT

With Holt's sleep schedule resembling that of a nocturnal creature, his bedroom needed to be a place where he could hole up and get some much needed downtime—whether it happened to be 2 a.m. or 2 p.m. So I wanted to make the space feel like a cozy man den of sorts. The main issue, however, was the room's long, awkwardly narrow space. The shape dictated that everything in the room work on a lengthwise plane, including the bed. There was no spot to place it perpendicular to the wall without almost touching the opposite side of the room. So I flipped it, putting the long side against the wall. But I couldn't just leave it floating in the middle of the wall with nothing to ground it, so I bought two basic white bookshelves from Target and placed them on either end of the mattress. Then I readjusted the pillows to create a daybed-like effect. Remember, you always want your furniture placement to feel like a purposeful move, not a last resort.

A set of bohemian lamps was the perfect unexpected touch in this room. They kept an argyle wall and striped rug from feeling too buttoned-up preppy.

HOW-TO: ARGYLE WALL

WHAT YOU NEED

- Measuring tape
- Level
- Pencil
- 1 roll of 3-inch-wide blue painter's tape
- 1 roll of 3-inch-wide painter's tape in an alternate color
- 1 gallon of flat gray paint
- 1 gallon of flat moss green paint

STEP 1

Measure your wall horizontally and vertically. Divide it in half horizontally, drawing a straight line through the center of your wall with your level and pencil.

STEP 2

Then divide your wall vertically into eight equal sections, drawing a straight line from ceiling to floorboard. For the sake of organization, I name my vertical lines V1 through V7 moving left to right.

STEP 3

Pencils down! It's time to play a giant game of "connect the dots" with tape. Starting at the ceiling corner on the far left-hand wall, take your blue painter's tape, and tape a diagonal line that begins there and ends at the point where your horizontal line crosses V1.

STEP 4

Continue taping a zigzag from your horizontal line to the ceiling across the entire top half of your wall. So you'll connect the horizontal mark on V1 with the V2 ceiling point, the V2 ceiling point with the horizontal mark on V3, and so forth, until you end at the ceiling corner on the far right-hand wall.

STEP 5

Repeat Step 4, only this time on the bottom half of your wall. So starting at the floorboard on the far left-hand wall, tape a diagonal line that begins there and ends at the point where your horizontal line crosses V1. Continue across the wall connecting the horizontal mark on V1 with the V2 floorboard point, the V2 floorboard point with the horizontal mark on V3, and so forth, until you end at the floorboard on the far right-hand wall.

STEP 6

You're halfway there! You just need to do a bit more taping. Here's where you switch your tape color. (This will help keep things in perspective when painting, though the choice of switching is up to you.) Starting in the corner of the far left-hand wall—where your horizontal mark stops—tape a diagonal line that begins there and ends at the V1 ceiling point.

STEP 7

Continue taping a zigzag across the top half of your wall. So you'll connect the V1 ceiling point with the horizontal mark on V2, the horizontal mark on V2 with the V3 ceiling point, and so forth, until

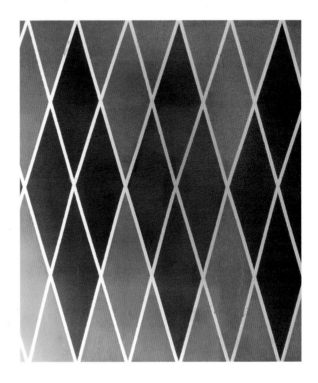

  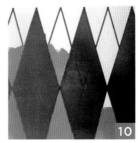 

you end on the far right-hand wall, where your horizontal mark stops.

STEP 8

Repeat Step 7 on the bottom half of your wall. Starting in the corner on the far left-hand wall—where your horizontal mark stops—tape a diagonal line that begins there and ends at the V1 floorboard point. Continue across the wall connecting the V1 floorboard point with the horizontal mark on V2, the horizontal mark on V2 with the V3 floorboard point, and so forth, until you

end in the far right-hand corner of the wall, where your horizontal mark stops.

STEP 9

Exhale. The hard part is over! You can break out the paint. Before you start, make sure all your tape is firmly pressed to the wall to deter any paint from seeping through and messing up all your hard work.

STEP 10

Your main diamonds—which will be painted gray—are taped off with your blue painter's tape. Apply two coats

of gray paint to the area inside these diamonds, and two coats of moss green to the area outside.

STEP 11

Let your paint dry for at least thirty to forty-five minutes before carefully removing the tape. You want the paint to be dry enough that it won't run but still a tad wet so that you have time to wipe off any paint that may have dripped into the white space. Let the paint sit overnight to dry.

THE ARGYLE COLOR CODE

Love the look but want to make it your own? Try these mood-setting color combos:

Feminine:
Plum, Cream, and Rose

Retro:
Chocolate, Burnt Orange, and Camel

Downtown:
Charcoal, Taupe, and Candy Apple Red

Neutral:
Tan, White, and Stone

Sleek:
Jet Black, Slate, and Dove Gray

"THE KEY TO PAINTING INTRICATE PATTERNS IS KEEPING THE SCALE LARGE."

CHEAT SHEET:
THE PREPPY

1
START WITH FABRIC, NOT PAINT, when decorating. You have the option of every color under the sun with paint. Fabric selection is much more limited—but also much more inspiring.

2
THE BOLDER—AND MORE DIVERSE—THE PRINTS, the richer the space, so don't be scared to layer multiple patterns in the same room.

3
BUYING A PIECE OF FURNITURE, whether old or new, is only the first step in making it your own. Add a personal touch whenever and wherever you can.

4
DON'T LET A CHOPPED-UP FLOOR PLAN GET YOU DOWN. Create distinct zones, and use the opportunity to embrace a few different aesthetics in your apartment.

5
FORM WILL FOLLOW FUNCTION, so decorate around how you actually use a space. A functional room will always be good design.

THE ROOMMATES

WHO: Anne & Julia

JOB: Corporate PR coordinator & financial services consultant

LIVE IN: Back Bay, Boston

MEASUREMENTS: 800 square feet

IN THE HIERARCHY OF ROOMMATE RELATIONSHIPS, ANNE AND JULIA ARE WHAT YOU'D CALL "LONG TERM."

The two met in college and moved in together after graduation. Three years and three apartments later, they finally landed in a spot where they could see themselves staying for a while. The small flat is located in one of the many nineteenth-century, federal-style brownstones-turned-apartment complexes in Boston's Back Bay neighborhood.

Anne and Julia loved having cool shops and restaurants right on their street. But that luxury came at a sacrifice: space. Their apartment was one long room with two small bedrooms. (If someone sneezed in the kitchen, it was heard in Julia's back bedroom.) But after spending two years commuting from roomy apartments in not-so-convenient neighborhoods, they decided their next move would be about finding the right location. Because the truth is: space and location are always going to be at opposite ends of the priority seesaw. The faster you decide which holds more weight for you, the happier you'll be with your living situation.

Anne likes bright colors and bold prints with a bohemian spin. Julia prefers neutral hues, clean lines, and a traditional coastal feel. Up until this point, Anne and Julia had never stayed put long enough to care how everything came together. But now they wanted their new apartment to reflect each of their personalities—and making that happen in a visually cohesive way became my job. With a color lover and a color-phobe under the same roof, decorating became a give-and-take negotiation with bright, surprisingly tranquil results.

MUSICAL CHAIRS

TIP: The mix-and-match approach to buying dining room chairs can save you hundreds of dollars. These were all purchased for around $60, whereas a matching set would have cost upwards of $200. If you want something more cohesive, simply paint your collection the same color.

As different as Anne and Julia's tastes may be, there was one unlikely source of inspiration they could both agree on: their favorite television show, *Friends.* (Cue the theme music.) They loved the colorful, mismatched chairs around the kitchen table in Monica's apartment, so I wanted to re-create that in a more modern way here. The table was originally pushed against the living room wall, and felt more like an afterthought. They didn't even have actual chairs for it, only folding ones that were kept stored until needed.

I hit the local thrift stores and started picking up the cheapest chairs I could find. Since I was planning on painting them, it didn't matter what sort of shape they were in as long as the frame was sturdy. I found two chairs with classic details and two that were a little more ornamental (one of which was technically a bench), then painted each a different color: turquoise, raspberry, tangerine, and dove gray. The result was a collection of seating that turned a sleek lacquer table into something far more eclectic—which was a better reflection of both girls' style.

THE FLOOR PLAN

The main living area in Anne and Julia's apartment was extra long and extra narrow, a less-than-ideal combination when trying to place a large sectional sofa. With a space like this, traffic flow has to take precedence; otherwise you end up with an obstacle course of furniture—which is what existed when I arrived. The sofa was flush with the bay window, and the kitchen table was positioned against the wall behind it. Everything felt cramped, which in turn made the room feel smaller.

Breaking up the furniture gridlock—placing the round table in front of the bay windows and sliding the sofa down the wall—made both the "living room" and "kitchen" areas feel bigger and gave the whole room a more natural course. Don't get caught up in where you think something belongs. Let your space dictate function, and place things where they work.

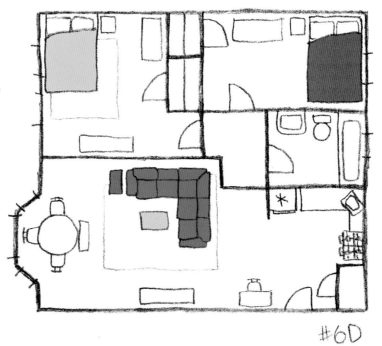

#6D

A LITTLE GIVE, A LITTLE TAKE

In an attempt to appease each other's design aesthetic, the "living room" area had become a watered-down version of both roommates' styles—with neither one really loving anything about the space. But here's the thing: if one roommate likes blue and the other likes red, purple is never the answer. Communal decorating shouldn't feel like a debate, nor should it be a total abandonment of personal style. Instead, think of it as a game of something for everyone, with a few veto clauses thrown in for good measure. Here, we created a checklist of sorts: the streamlined sofa was Julia's style, the chevron carpet tiles were Anne's, the colonial side table was Julia's, the industrial reading lamp was Anne's, and so forth. Decorating was a piece-by-piece addition of something each one really loved, which made the whole room feel so much more alive.

SOUND OFF

Like most old apartments, this one had a big problem with echoes, especially in the main room, which at times felt like a noise tunnel. The chevron carpet tiles we installed helped a bit, but I wanted to do something that would absorb the reverb from the walls—so I turned it into an art project. The landlord wouldn't let us paint. (She barely allowed us to use nails.) So I came up with the idea of creating fabric-covered, padded panels that would Velcro onto the wall as a way to add color and solve the sound issue (see page 92 for details on making your own). Anne chose a bright yellow fabric, and Julia opted for a subtle stripe. I did a checkerboard effect with the panels across both walls, which acted as the perfect substitute for artwork—saving me money and the daunting task of finding something Anne and Julia could agree on. Afterward, the sound wasn't completely snuffed out, but the muffled noise escaping from the living room was far more bearable.

TIP: Think of the floor as your fifth wall, and use it to display bold prints or colors.

A QUICK NOTE ON: INSTALLING FLOR CARPET TILES

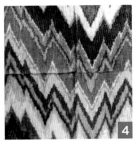

STEP 1: Line up your FLOR Tiles where you want them. **STEP 2:** Starting with a corner tile, attach one-quarter of a FLOR Dot (which come with your purchase) to an inside corner of your tile. **STEP 3:** Keep your stickered FLOR Tile straight, and attach each of the 3 tiles that border it. Repeat this step while working your way to the opposite end of your FLOR Tile rug. **STEP 4:** Once the inside is completely connected, make your way around the perimeter, connecting one tile to the next, using half a FLOR Dot on each edge.

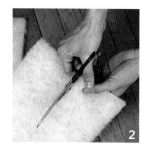

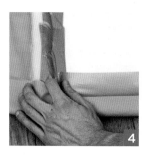

HOW-TO: PADDED FABRIC PANELS

WHAT YOU NEED

- Fabric
- 36- by 48-inch foam core board
- Scissors
- 1 roll of batting
- Duct tape
- 1 roll of industrial-strength Velcro Sticky Back tape
- Painter's tape

....

STEP 1

Cut your fabric to fit your foam core board, leaving an extra 2-inch border around the edges.

STEP 2

Cut your batting to the size of your foam core board, this time leaving an extra 1-inch border around the edge.

STEP 3

Lay your batting on a flat surface, and line up your foam core board on top, making sure the extra inch you cut is even all the way around. Fold the extra batting over the edge of your board, and duct tape it down. You want it to be as flush with the surface of your board as possible.

STEP 4

Lay your fabric on a flat surface and line up your batting-covered foam core board on top—batting side down—again making sure the extra 2 inches of material you left is even all the way around. Wrap your fabric over the edge one side at a time—top then bottom, right then left—and duct tape it to the back of your foam core board. Treat the corners the way you would if you were wrapping a gift. (You want your fabric taut, but not so tight it bunches or pulls.)

STEP 5

Cut four, 3-inch squares from your roll of Sticky Back Velcro tape. Place one square in each of the four corners on the back of your foam core board.

STEP 6

Decide where you want to hang your fabric-covered foam core board. In pencil, mark the four spaces on the wall that line up with the Velcro squares on your board. Cover these areas in blue painter's tape.

STEP 7

Pull off the top piece of the Velcro squares attached to your foam core board. Stick one square to each of the areas covered in blue painter's tape, making sure they line up with the Velcro squares on the back of your board.

STEP 8

Firmly press your fabric-covered foam core board to the wall and, *voilà,* your panel is hung without using a single nail.

"DON'T GET TRAPPED BY A COLOR YOU DON'T LOVE; THERE IS ALWAYS A WAY TO TEMPER IT."

THE BEAUTY AISLE

Two girls and one small bathroom equals a whole lot of beauty products scattered around. The tub was lined with bottles, the sink framed by makeup, there were even a few rogue liquid soap containers on the floor outside the shower. The goal here was to give each roommate her own personal area—for the sake of storage and organization. There was an oversized ledge in the shower, so I bought two indoor/outdoor waterproof wicker baskets, which became a catchall for Anne and Julia's shower products. Then we instituted a new rule: if it doesn't fit in the basket, it doesn't stay in the bathroom. This was the only way to keep the space somewhat organized.

NOT SO PRETTY IN PINK

The pale pink tile that lined the bathroom wall reminded Julia of her great-grandmother's house (not in a good way)—and Anne had some serious aversions to it as well. So I wanted to introduce some darker colors to make it feel a little less dated. I swapped their plain white shower curtain for one that had graphic silhouettes all over it. Then I hung some art on the wall that Anne had painted when she was still in college. In the end, the pink tile became a background to all these bold new elements. Don't ever get trapped by a color you don't love; there is always a way to temper it.

To eliminate the ongoing game of "which towel is mine?" I gave each roommate a new set of towels in her very own color: plum or mauve.

BOHEMIAN NIGHTS

The bedrooms were the one place that Anne and Julia could freely decorate according to their own vision—no watering down or sharing necessary. So I really wanted each to be a personal retreat that made all the give-and-take in the rest of the apartment worthwhile.

In Anne's room, that meant playing up her love of eclectic, bohemian prints and accents. Hers was the smaller of the two rooms, with just enough square footage to fit a full-size bed, large dresser, and side table. It was so narrow, in fact, that both ends of her mattress were already flush with the wall, leaving no space for a proper headboard. To make the bed feel more substantial, we faked a traditional colonial headboard with a decorative wall decal that, come moving day, could be peeled right off without damaging the paint—which fell within the constraints of her landlord's rules.

Then we dotted the room with small personal touches: the black knobs that came on her Ikea dresser were switched for floral ones from Anthropologie (Anne's favorite store), and lots of earthy accents were added, like a woven basket for books, a sisal rug, and a reading lamp covered in captured butterflies. Sometimes the smallest details tell the most compelling story, so don't get stuck looking for that one, expensive statement piece—a lot of special little things work just as well.

TIP: Always opt for a reversible comforter; you can flip it over if you ever get tired of one side. So technically, you're getting double the print for the price of one.

HOW-TO: KNOB MAKEOVER

I've said it before, but it's certainly worth repeating: whenever you can personalize a store-bought piece, you should. You can probably find this Ikea dresser in over a million homes around the world. It's one of those "it does the job" pieces, but that doesn't mean it has to be boring. Switching out the manufacturer's knobs for something with more personality cost about $50 and took less than five minutes. Simply unscrew the old knobs and screw on the new.

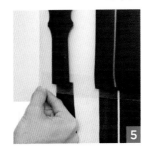

HOW-TO: INSTALLING A HEADBOARD DECAL

WHAT YOU NEED

- Olivia Headboard Blik Wall Decal (comes in two parts)
- 1 willing set of extra hands
- 1 plastic card or squeegee

STEP 1

Unroll the bottom half of your decal on the floor, clear side facing down. Pull the white backing off one of the bottom corners of your decal.

STEP 2

Carefully line up this corner of your decal with the floorboard. You're staging the placement of the headboard decal, so be sure to take your time and line it up exactly where you want it.

STEP 3

Enlist your buddy to hold up the other end of your decal. Start pulling off more of the white backing, while continuing to stick the clear portion directly to the wall. Be sure to keep this as straight as possible, until all the white backing is removed and the bottom portion is fully stuck to the wall.

STEP 4

Use your plastic card or squeegee to smooth out any wrinkles or air bubbles that may be left between your decal and the wall, especially under the part of the decal that is the headboard.

STEP 5

Repeat Steps 1 through 4 with the top half of your headboard decal, only this time, line up the top decal with the bottom portion already on the wall.

STEP 6

Once both pieces of your decal are on the wall and air bubble free, slowly start peeling off the clear plastic film on top—leaving only the headboard silhouette on the wall. If some of the headboard starts to peel off too, gently use your plastic card, squeegee, or finger to stick it back on the wall.

> " WHEN YOU DON'T HAVE A LOT TO SPEND, DEDICATE YOUR MONEY TO MAKING A BIG IMPACT IN A SPECIFIC AREA. "

NIGHT BLOOMERS

Julia's room was slightly larger with lots of natural light thanks to two windows overlooking a courtyard out back. Space-wise, it was plenty big for the usual bedroom necessities. The problem was, Julia didn't like any of the hand-me-down pieces that filled her bedroom. Nothing felt like "her" because technically it wasn't anything she would have picked out for herself. We didn't have the budget to start over again from scratch, unfortunately, but we could revamp some of the larger pieces and replace some of the smaller ones, like her dated bedding. When you don't have a lot to spend, it's always wise to dedicate your money to making an impact in a specific area.

I focused all of my attention on Julia's bed and the walls around it. We found a new duvet on clearance that slid right over her old comforter, which was much cheaper than buying a whole new quilt. Then I made a canvas slipcover to hide the winding, black, 1990's wrought iron bed frame that stood out in Julia's all-neutral room (see page 103 for instructions on making your own headboard slipcover). Those two changes alone were enough to create the calm, coastal vibe that Julia wanted. But I felt like she needed something truly unique to finish off her space, so we made an art installation of sorts using a single packet of Umbra wall flowers from Bed Bath & Beyond. These are so great; they come in different sizes and clip right onto a small thumbtack-size post, so you're barely leaving a hole in the wall. We wrapped them around the corner above her headboard, which gave the wall this beautiful, three-dimensional effect—and the whole project cost about $20.

The trick to making neutral bedding interesting? Just add texture. The woven check on this throw pillow breaks up the repeating larger check of the comforter perfectly.

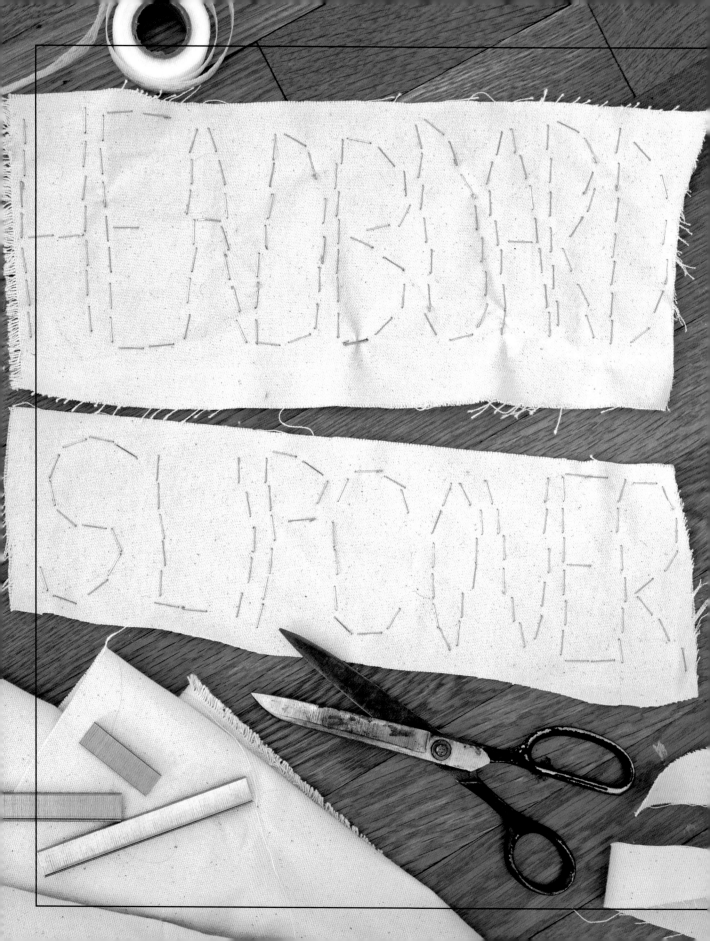

HOW-TO: HEADBOARD SLIPCOVER

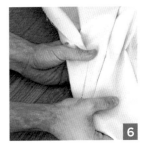

WHAT YOU NEED

- Measuring tape
- Heavy-duty canvas
- Scissors
- 1 roll, 1-inch Stitch Witchery regular tape
- Iron
- Stapler
- Staples

STEP 1

Measure and cut your heavy-duty canvas, so you have five pieces total: one front, one back, two sides, and a top. Base your measurements on the distance from the top of the headboard to where your box spring ends; the distance from post to post; and the depth of your headboard at its widest point—then add 2 extra inches to each measurement.

STEP 2

Line up all five pieces on the floor for assembly. Place your top piece in the center, flanked by the front and back on both of its long sides, and your two side pieces on either of its short ends (see illustration below).

STEP 3

Cut four strips of Stitch Witchery to match the length of each side of your top piece.

STEP 4

Stack your front piece on your top piece, and line up the corresponding outer edges so they are flush. Place a strip of Stitch Witchery along the edge between the two, and press down with your iron on the highest setting for five minutes.

STEP 5

Repeat Step 4 for your back and two side pieces, allowing the tape to cool for five minutes before moving the pieces.

STEP 6

Using the same technique as above, connect the four remaining sides of your headboard. (Just be extra careful that all your finished seams stay on the same side.)

STEP 7

At this point, you should have an inside-out headboard with your seams still visible. Because we're using heavy-duty fabric, you want to reinforce the Stitch Witchery seams. Take your stapler and staple along the outer edge of each seam.

STEP 8

Flip your slipcover inside out, and you should have a headboard that's ready to slide right over your existing one.

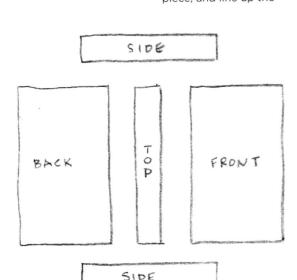

CHEAT SHEET:
THE ROOMMATES

1

CO-DECORATING ISN'T ABOUT COMPROMISING PERSONAL TASTE; it's about give-and-take, so everyone gets something to love.

2

WHEN YOUR WALLS ARE OFF LIMITS, think of your floor as the fifth wall, and have fun with rugs in bright colors and prints.

3

ORGANIZATION IS THE KEY to an argument-free household. In rooms as easily cluttered as a bathroom, everything should have a place.

4

A COLLECTION OF MISMATCHED CHAIRS is infinitely more interesting than a store-bought set—and a fraction of the cost.

5

TRY UPDATING WHAT YOU HAVE before splurging on something new—it's always worth a shot, especially if you're at the point of tossing something out anyway.

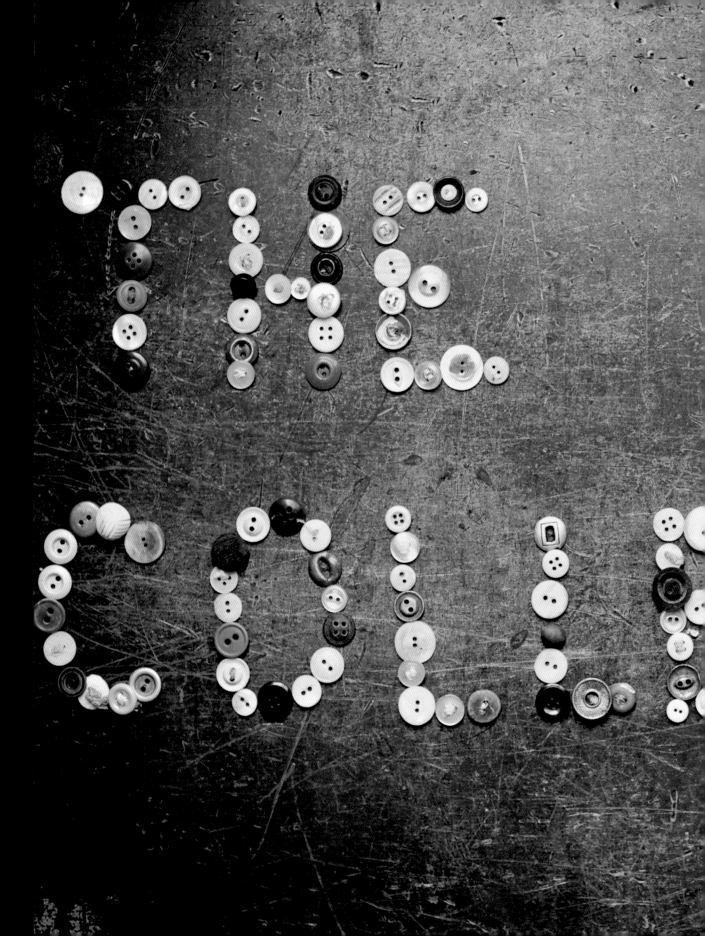

THE COLLECTOR

WHO: Jacob

JOB: Photographer

LIVES IN: Los Feliz, LA

MEASUREMENTS:
775 square feet

JACOB HAS AN EYE FOR COOL, OFF-THE-WALL DETAILS. IT'S PART OF THE REASON HE BECAME A PHOTOGRAPHER.

And it's also part of what piqued his interest in this classic, gothic-style apartment building in LA's Los Feliz neighborhood. The one-bedroom unit he lives in is small with a choppy layout, but the architectural quirks and old-timey features (rounded doorways, arched windows) are what really sold him on it—never mind that up until a decade ago the building was vacant and home to a community of squatters. He considered the grungy history to be part of the charm. It also didn't hurt that the landlord, though really strict about what he could do in the way of décor, had invested a lot into the freshly renovated building. He'd painted all the walls, for instance, so painting over them was absolutely forbidden.

Jacob moved in with a library's worth of art books, all his photo equipment, and a massive assortment of collections, which included everything from glass bottles to ceramic German shepherds (that at last count numbered in the hundreds). Add to that his loving (but rambunctious) Rottweiler, Parker, and you have a pretty full house. You see, though Jacob prefers the term "collector," his ability to stockpile things, like vintage tennis racquets from the 1940s, fell somewhere between being eccentric and borderline hoarding. And though possession-wise he owned a lot, it unfortunately did not include any major pieces of furniture other than an inherited sofa and his childhood bed frame—which meant there were no surfaces on which to arrange all the little bits and pieces that mattered most to Jacob. So my goal was clear: divide, conquer, and display.

DOG DAYS OF DECORATING

Man's best friend, sadly, is furniture's worst enemy. What they don't chew, they shed on. (But they're so darn cute, it's worth it, right?) Jacob's Rottweiler, Parker, couldn't have been sweeter, but at 70 pounds it was like having a second person living in an already tiny space. The trick to not letting your dog—or cat—destroy your apartment is decorating for them too. The reality is this: they will jump on your sofa, they will chew on table legs, and they will have accidents on the rug. But with a little pet proofing, you can tip the scales in your favor. Here are a few helpful tips:

- **Stick with furniture in either leather or microfiber, which is easier to clean.**
- **Industrial furniture—with metal legs—is the way to go. It won't stop your dog from chewing, but the damage the dog can inflict is minimal. (Plus, you want these pieces to look a little beaten up—it adds to the charm.)**
- **Buy rugs in natural woven materials like jute, which are not very absorbent and already have a lovingly worn-in look.**

THE FLOOR PLAN

Jacob needed his apartment to function as a live/work space, but he didn't have room for a proper office. So he was insistent that the "work" portion be designated to one specific area. Otherwise, he would be tempted to work straight through the night. What was great about this layout is that it divided the apartment up for him: the front half (living room and dining room) was where he could work and have meetings, while the back half (kitchen, bedroom, and bathroom) was separated off as personal space. Making the designation between "public" and "private" areas was essential for Jacob's finding a happy work/life balance.

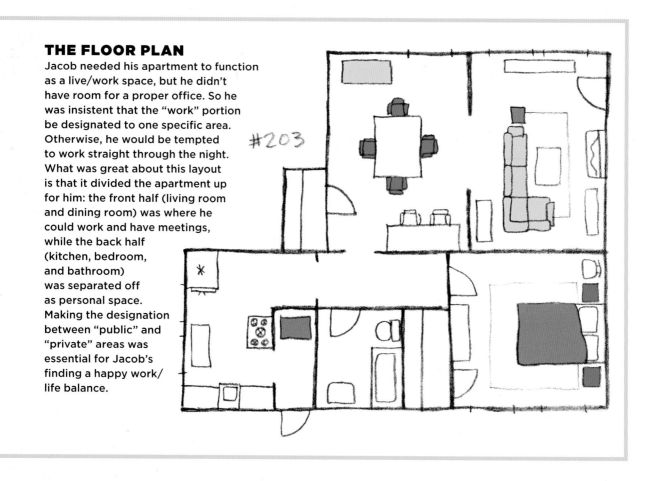

"THINK OF A VIGNETTE AS YOUR OWN PERSONAL TOOL FOR CONTROLLING WHERE PEOPLE'S ATTENTION GOES IN A ROOM—AND USE IT WISELY."

Richard Billingham Ray's a laugh

THE WHITE OAK DANCE PROJECT PHOTOGRAPHED BY ANNIE LEIBOVITZ
M. SASEK

The Photographs of Ron Galella

ON DISPLAY

Jacob's collections were overwhelming him. Instead of finding creative ways to showcase everything, he gave up. He grouped each set of items together in a single place, which resulted in an apartment that looked as if it belonged to an eccentric old lady. The trick to chasing away the granny element? Organizing his collections into small vignettes, and then spreading them across the entire apartment. Since each vignette included a few pieces from each collection, every room felt like it had a little personal touch.

THE DINING ROOM OFFICE

Jacob spent most days shooting on location, but he did all of his pre- and post-production work from home. That meant he not only needed workspace for himself but also for two to three interns on a regular basis. Between the head count and the equipment, a decent amount of square footage was needed—which is why he knew the second he saw this dining room that he'd turn it into an office. That said, its central location—you had to walk through the dining room to get from one end of the apartment to the other—posed a bit of a problem.

Jacob didn't want the room to be lined with desks. So I did my best to give it an office-undercover vibe: it looked like your basic dining room, but functionality-wise it was built for work. The wooden table was a little wider than normal, so up to four people could comfortably work on it, laptops and all. And since Jacob had access to heavy-duty industrial pieces used at most photo studios, I was able to get an inexpensive metal locker that was about the size of your typical buffet sideboard. Instead of filling the locker with dishes though, I put scanners, a printer, laptops, and all the other equipment Jacob and his team used inside. The key here was looking for work-friendly versions of what you'd expect to find in a dining room, so that when you do want to have a meal at the table, you won't feel like you're eating at your desk.

BOTTLENECK

An empty table always feels a little sad to me. But most twenty-somethings can't splurge on fresh flower arrangements every week. The next best thing: a grouping of little items, like these bottles. Jacob had over two dozen clear bottles stashed under his kitchen sink. (Another of his collections.) To make them feel more cohesive, I picked eight bottles in varying shapes and sizes and painted them the same shade of opaque eggshell (see page 117 for details on making your own painted bottles). Then I displayed them on an organic-feeling wooden cutting board. In the end, the assortment of bottles felt modern and a little earthy too.

Since Jacob needed extremely versatile chairs—sometimes all six were around the table, other times they were pulled into the living room—we opted for a style without arms, which take up less space visually and work in a variety of situations.

HOW-TO: PAINTED BOTTLES

WHAT YOU NEED
- Clear bottles (cleaned)
- 1, 8-ounce squeeze bottle of acrylic paint
- 1 roll of paper towels
- Wax paper
- Cookie sheet

STEP 1
Squeeze 1 tablespoon of paint into a bottle.

STEP 2
Add two drops of water to your paint—you want to loosen it up, not make it watery.

STEP 3
Cover your thumb with a paper towel, and then cork the bottle. Start shaking! The paint should coat the entire inside.

STEP 4
Play with your technique: roll the bottle to get paint into tricky spots, or add a drop of water if it's still too thick. (But not too much or the paint will streak.)

STEP 5
Turn the bottle upside down to dry on a wax paper–covered cookie sheet. Let sit for three hours before moving.

(Note: These bottles can't be used as vases. Adding water will dilute the paint and cause it to peel.)

EMBRACE THE OLD

Jacob's apartment had a rustic-industrial, slightly menswearish aesthetic. However, the second you stepped into his kitchen, it felt like you'd been transported to the 1950s. There was faded yellow tile work, a restored O'Keefe & Merritt stove, even a built-in (nonfunctioning) icebox on the wall. The kitchen clearly didn't go with the rest of the apartment, but the truth of the situation was this: there was absolutely nothing we could do about it. Painting was forbidden, and any other wide-scale overhauls would have cost major bucks.

Instead of filling the kitchen with modern touches to try and balance the old-school vibe, I convinced Jacob to embrace it. When faced with a room that is obviously one aesthetic—in this case, a kitchen that belongs on the set of *The Wonder Years*—filling it with things that are so far outside that vibe will often make the difference even more pronounced. So we looked for retro-designed appliances, like the yellow toaster from Target.com, on his countertop, and the vintage 1970s dishes—swiped from his parents' house. Then I turned that nonworking icebox into a fully functioning bar for when Jacob had parties. The whole space still felt very yesteryear, but thanks to all the little touches, it was old in a very cool way.

TIP: Hanging artwork above a stove is tricky—you're dealing with an open flame and grease nearby. So we set one of Jacob's own photos between two pieces of plexiglass. It wipes clean (essential in an area where you're cooking), and most important, the plexiglass is less of a fire hazard than, say, a wooden frame.

A LESSON IN DIVISION

Within Jacob's vast collection of ceramic German shepherds, there were smaller subcollections, like this section of all-white figurines. I wanted to highlight the great details in this group, so instead of including them in the vignettes I created earlier, I kept them intact and displayed them together—mixing in a few darker statuettes to break it up just a bit. Since aesthetically they shared so many similarities, I could get away with arranging a large group together without its feeling too chaotic. Look for chances to make subcollections within your own collections; it's the perfect way to get people interested in something you've spent a lot of time building.

BOTTOM RIGHT: The back door off this alcove leads to a little play area for Parker. I wanted to make it more functional, so I added two very small hooks to the wall where Jacob could hang his hoodies.

SLEEPING QUARTERS

Jacob's bedroom felt more like a sleeping closet. Luckily, it was big enough to fit a full-size bed and two side tables, but the space stopped there. That's the tricky thing about small bedrooms . . . the furniture you need to fill them with is always large, so your small room inevitably feels smaller. But there's one thing to remember when dealing with tight spaces: lines are your best friend. They automatically create the illusion of length. So in Jacob's room, I included a tight pinstripe on the bed, which was echoed again in the throw pillows. Then I used thirty carpet tiles to create a patchwork effect on the floor. The stripes on the bed made the room feel wider, while the stripes of the floor made it feel longer.

To give the illusion of even more space, I played around with mirrors and the room's natural light. Jacob's bed frame, the same one he had slept in since he was thirteen years old, sits a tad higher off the floor than most—which worked out to our advantage. Forgoing a dust ruffle and keeping the bedding nice and tidy (check out those sharp hospital corners) decreased the amount of space the bed took up visually.

For the same reason, we chose side tables with shelves instead of drawers, which let the sunlight seep into all the dark corners. Then I turned a set of his vintage tennis racquets into a really cool installation of mirrors above his bed, since mirrors always add depth to a room. (See page 123 for details on making your own tennis racquet mirrors.) With a little design trickery, Jacob's small bedroom actually felt perfectly comfortable—even slightly roomy.

(See page 123 for details on making your own tennis racquet mirrors.)

TIP: Opt for carpet tiles under large pieces of furniture, like a bed, instead of a rug. Since you need to trace only the perimeter of your piece with tiles—and you can leave the underneath portion bare—it ends up costing half as much as a large rug. Plus, carpet tiles are easy to replace if your dog has an accident.

Every room deserves a little greenery, so I added a succulent to this side table. This plant is pet-friendly (and owner-proof). You can go two weeks without watering it.

HOW-TO: MIRRORED TENNIS RACQUETS

WHAT YOU NEED
- 5 tennis racquets
- 5 custom-cut mirrors
- 2-ounce bottle of Gorilla Glue
- 5 D-ring metal picture hanger kits (with screws)

STEP 1
Take your tennis racquets to the local glass and mirror store, and have mirrors cut to fit each one. You can either purchase the mirrors there, or if you bring your own mirrors, it should cost about $10 per cut.

STEP 2
Decide which side of your racquet you'd like to be on display, then place your mirror on top of the racquet strings on that side. On the back side, trace the strings of the tennis racquet with your Gorilla Glue, making sure to hold the mirror firmly against the strings.

STEP 3
Continue pressing your mirror firmly to the strings until the glue is set—about five minutes. You'll know it's set when the glue turns from clear to milky white.

STEP 4
Screw your D-ring metal picture hanger directly into your racquet. Placement will depend on how you want it to hang. Here, all the hooks are screwed into the same place in the center of the racquet,

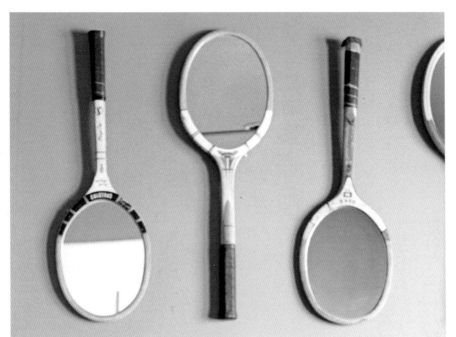

but they are alternated according to the side of the racquet that will point toward the ceiling or floor.

LOVE THIS LOOK?

Here's a list of more vintage sporting equipment that happens to look great displayed on a wall.

- Archery Arrows
- Snow Skis
- Rowing Oars
- Cricket Bats
- Fly Fishing Poles

THE CURATED CORNER

For a rental, Jacob had a surprisingly large bathroom, which included the luxury of a tub and shower—though the tub was enjoyed far more by Parker. There was even a small window in the corner that let in a little natural light. But like the kitchen, the bathroom was stuck in a bygone decade. The yellow tile was framed in Kelly green, and all the fixtures felt like they were from the 1960s.

The landlord had painted the wall a pale gray, which thankfully felt a little modern, but we needed to add a few more touches to make the space seem more masculine. So I introduced some woodsy elements, like rattan window shades, a set of reclaimed railroad tie shelves, and a postcard board I made from a selection of cards Jacob had compiled during his years of traveling. (See page 127 for details on making your own postcard board.) The rustic touches balanced out the dated elements, while adding a retro summer camp vibe.

OPPOSITE: When you only have a pedestal sink, try adding a simple cabinet (if there's room). Not only will it give you storage, but it's also a second countertop that you can use for toiletries.

HOW-TO: POSTCARD BOARD

WHAT YOU NEED

- 1 piece of wood
- Hairdryer (optional)
- 32-ounce bottle of Mod Podge Matte
- 3-inch-wide paintbrush
- Collection of postcards
- 1 wire picture hanging kit
- 1 screwdriver

STEP 1
Clean your piece of wood with water and soap, and let it dry completely. (You can use a hairdryer to speed up the process.)

STEP 2
Apply a liberal coat of Mod Podge to the top of your piece of wood with a 3-inch brush. You want the top to be thickly covered, but not runny.

STEP 3
Arrange your postcards however you like. Don't rush; you have about fifteen minutes to play around with placement before your first coat of Mod Podge gets too dry to pick up the postcards.

STEP 4
Once everything is as you want it, apply another coat of Mod Podge over the top of the postcards—you're basically sealing the postcards to the wood. You'll want to apply at least two or three more coats of Mod Podge, allowing about twenty-five minutes of drying time between coats.

STEP 5
Screw your wire picture hanging hooks into the back of your piece of wood. Then you're ready to hang it!

CHEAT SHEET:
THE COLLECTOR

1

USE INDUSTRIAL PIECES when decorating for pets. It's a great way to turn the "worn and weathered look" into a positive.

2

INSTEAD OF GROUPING YOUR COLLECTIONS all together, spread them around your space. It gives your eye a place to rest (and appreciate) what's on display.

3

USE STRIPED ACCENTS going in various directions to make tight spaces feel bigger.

4

TURN YOUR COLLECTIONS INTO something functional—not just visual—as we did with the mirrored tennis racquets.

5

TAKE A STROLL THROUGH YOUR FAVORITE—inexpensive—vintage store for inspiration. Then find something similar and cheaper on eBay.

the
scholar

THE SCHOLAR

WHO: Julie

JOB: Teacher

LIVES IN: Bucktown, Chicago

MEASUREMENTS: 600 square feet

ASK ANY ONE OF JULIE'S LEGION OF FRIENDS WHAT HER MOTTO SHOULD BE, AND YOU'LL GET SOME VERSION OF "ALWAYS HAPPY TO HELP" AS YOUR ANSWER.

The Chicago native has logged six years with the Teach for America program. She just returned from a year-long trip to Peru, where she volunteered at an elementary school. And she's the go-to person to call when any of her friends find themselves in a bind. But as is the case with most selfless people, Julie takes no time for herself. She chose her one-bedroom, Bucktown flat strictly out of convenience to the closest El train stop. Between teaching Spanish at an inner-city school, studying for her master's, and juggling volunteer work, she's barely unpacked. Did she want a perfectly put together apartment? Sure. Was it at the top of her priority list? Not even close.

Here's what most superbusy folks don't realize though: taking two days to turn your bare-bones apartment into a happily decorated home is a huge time-saver in the long run. Afterward, everything has its place, so you can come home and just relax—and if anyone deserves that luxury, it's Julie. After rent, tuition, and bills were paid, her teacher's salary didn't leave much spending cash. Her apartment consisted of the purely functional furniture basics (the result of a raid on her parents' basement) and none of the personal "extras"—those little things that make a space feel like home. So it was time for this multitasking teacher to take a lesson in the art of the final touch.

MELLOW YELLOW

TIP: Julie's hand-me-down sofa is actually the two end pieces of a larger sectional. The middle piece made the sofa too large for the room, so I got rid of it. A sectional opens up the possibilities of customizing seating to fit your space, so if you have one make sure you're taking advantage.

Julie's living room was what I like to call "beige camouflage." There was a beige sofa against a beige brick wall on a tan wood floor. This room was in desperate need of definition and color. But the landlord wouldn't let us paint or put a single hole in the brick wall. It needed to be broken up visually, though, so I created my own exposed wood beams using 1- by 4-foot wood planks, bright yellow paint, and some industrial-strength Velcro for attaching them to the brick without causing permanent holes (see page 92 for instructions on attaching items to the wall with Velcro).

Spreading pops of color across the wall gave the eye a place to rest—and drew attention to Julie's 9-foot ceilings. (You can do this treatment on any wall surface.) It also gave the option of hanging something—now that we had a spot to hammer in a nail—so I placed a papier-mâché gazelle bust above the sofa. Then I worked bold, brown-and-ivory patterns into the room with a rug and decorative Peruvian bowl. The roots of this space are still beige, but these small, impactful additions turned a neutral room into something far more rich and diverse.

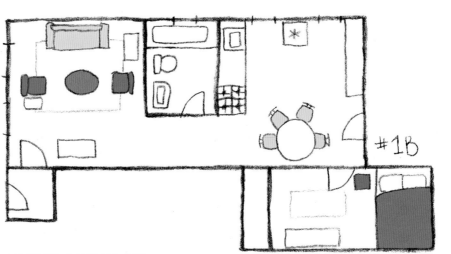

THE FLOOR PLAN

Julie's apartment was shaped like an elongated U, with the bathroom as the carved-out center—and the bedroom hanging off the back like an afterthought. She had a definite living room and a definite kitchen, but the hallway that connected the two was abnormally wide. Julie's first instinct was to leave this area open, but by doing so, she was dwarfing her two main living areas—and breaking the cardinal rule of small apartment living: never waste space! So I rotated the entertainment center in her living room into the hallway—which opened up the seating area. Then I moved her dining table from the center of the kitchen to the hallway wall, giving her the option of folding the table's leaves up for more surface area. These simple adjustments made Julie's apartment feel almost twice as large.

STENCIL
WALL,
P. 139

SPORTS CENTER

Come baseball season, White Sox games at Julie's apartment are a weekly affair. (Everyone brings a dish and gathers round the flat screen.) This played a major factor in how I laid out the furniture in this room. Originally, Julie had the entertainment center in front of the window, the sofa on the far wall, and the two chairs against the brick. This configuration meant the entertainment center was the focal point of the whole room. But you never want your living room to feel like a TV room because when it does, all you do in there is watch television. So when I rotated the entertainment center into the hallway, instead of placing everything in a semicircle facing it, I created an intimate, conversation-friendly layout with the area rug as my centering element. It opened up the space to so many more activities, while still giving every seat an unobstructed view of the television on game day.

TIP: If you're worried about painting over a wall when you move out, opt for lighter shades that will only take one coat of paint to cover up again.

COLORING WITHIN THE LINES

The landlord's opinion on wall paint was pretty much the norm: if you paint it, you have to paint it back. Since Julie wasn't sure how long she was going to be in this apartment, she didn't want to commit to anything that would be too much of a hassle when move-out time came. So I picked two accent walls to paint, one in the living room and one in the bedroom. To add more pattern and more color, I used a graphic stencil across the entire living room wall, echoing the same yellow from my wood beams. It lightened up the mood of the space with one bold kick.

" THE CARDINAL RULE OF SMALL APARTMENT LIVING: NEVER WASTE SPACE!"

Julie's bookcase was loaded with unattractive textbooks and teacher manuals. Instead of leaving the tattered spines facing the room, I flipped them around so the space got this really great texture that was also visually cohesive color-wise.

HOW-TO: STENCIL WALL

WHAT YOU NEED

- 3 stencil sheets*
- Level
- Painter's tape
- Acrylic paint
- Mini-paint roller

STEP 1

Tape your first stencil sheet to the top corner of the wall. Use the wall and ceiling as a guide, but double-check that your pattern is level before moving forward. Once you're sure it's straight, attach the stencil to the wall with painter's tape.

STEP 2

Most stencils have guides along the corners that make it easy to match up your next stencil sheet—which ensures that the repeat of your pattern is consistent. Mine had small triangles, so I worked my way down the wall taping my other 2 stencil sheets in place once they were accurately lined up.

STEP 3

Paint the area covered by your first 3 stencil sheets. It's easy for paint to drip underneath your stencil, so make sure your roller has very little paint on it. Let the area dry for ten minutes, and apply a second coat if necessary.

STEP 4

Carefully remove the top 2 stencil sheets from your wall, leaving the bottom one in place as a guide. Use your remaining stencil to line up your 2 stencil sheets below it; then remove it from the wall, and add it to the bottom of the stencil sheet chain—add paint as you did in the previous step. Continue working your way down the wall like so until you reach the floorboard.

STEP 5

Work your way across the wall, repeating Steps 1 through 4. Double-check that each top stencil is level before adding paint, and make sure your pattern continues to match up along the way.

*Technically, you only need 1 stencil sheet. But the more you have, the less time you'll spend taping and checking that everything is level.

"NEVER BUY SOMETHING NEW WITHOUT REEVALUATING HOW YOU'RE USING THE PIECES YOU ALREADY OWN."

THE ULTIMATE MULTITASKER

Julie was using a counter-height table with matching stools as an island in the center of her kitchen. She loves to cook, and it worked perfectly as a prep station. It did not, however, work so well as a place to eat. With all its flaps extended, the table was round with plenty of space to seat four. But in order to squeeze the table into the center of the kitchen, the flaps had to be kept down. So the spacious circle became an extremely narrow rectangle, which was impossible to sit at without bumping your knees on the folded-down sides.

As much as Julie enjoyed having the extra space for cooking, what she really needed was a multipurpose place to eat, study, and grade papers—something that was at the top of her makeover wish list. By moving the counter-height table against the hallway wall outside her bedroom, it became much more versatile—and was still close enough to the stove for Julie to prep food on it. Never buy something new without reevaluating how you're using the pieces you already own. If we'd given Julie what she initially wanted—a second table in the kitchen—we would have ended up with two even though one did the job of both just fine.

RUSTIC DINING

I'm convinced stools were never meant for long-term sitting—they can be so darn uncomfortable. Now that Julie was constantly parked at her table, she needed chairs she could spend a few hours in without parts of her body starting to spasm. So I traded in her stools for a set of proper counter chairs with comfortably high backs. There was, however, an ulterior motive to the switch: breaking up her matching dining set. It's one thing to inherit your great-grandmother's banquet table and chairs, and quite another to simply click and buy a prematched set on Ikea.com. Where does your personality come through? These new chairs have a rustic, French country aesthetic that made Julie's big-box-store table feel like it could have been a great vintage find. I'm not saying you shouldn't buy from a store like Target or Ikea—you absolutely should. But look around, take your time, mix and match, and make your purchase your own.

LE PETIT BISTRO

Located not even a full block from Julie's front door was a small sliver of a restaurant that served some of the city's best tapas and Spanish wine. It has only 16 seats at a thin bar—and at least once a week you could find Julie in one of those coveted spots. She loved the food as much as the cozy, European bistro-style atmosphere, with its subway tile walls, hanging wineglass displays, and flickering candlelight. The space was simple and romantic, so it didn't surprise me that when I asked what her ideal kitchen would look like Julie's response was . . . this restaurant. Funny thing though, she already had the framework in place to make that happen: white tile walls, natural lighting, even a spot to attach a fixture and hang wineglasses. Julie just didn't see it. It's easy to miss the potential of a room when it's lost in a sea of white. But if you focus on the details, you'll find the real personality.

I wanted to draw attention to those characteristics that felt like the restaurant Julie already loved, so I added strategic hits of black around the room: the inset fronts of the cabinets, the refrigerator doors, and in the graphic pattern of the curtains. Then I hung a 99-cent metal fixture above her sink for wineglasses. It took three quick, easy updates and a total of $250 to turn Julie's white-washed kitchen into a doppelganger of her favorite restaurant.

PLEASE REPORT TO THE BOARD

Kitchen cabinets are the eyesore of most rentals, since more often than not, they're simply the cheapest thing the landlord could find. The sad thing is: there's very little you can do to drastically change the look of cheap cabinets. Your options are limited to removing the doors completely (as we did on page 28), leaving your dishes exposed, or adding a temporary decal, as we did here. In either case, the goal is hiding the shoddy finish of the cabinet fronts.

In Julie's kitchen, I applied chalkboard decals to the inset center of her ten cabinet doors—and repeated the same treatment on the front of the refrigerator (see page 145 for instructions on making your own chalkboard fridge). I also swapped out her plastic white door handles for stainless steel knobs. These simple additions made her run-of-the-mill cabinet unit feel much more streamlined and expensive looking. Plus, she now has a built-in sketchpad for jotting off grocery lists, recipes, or good ol' procrastination doodles.

>> SECRET SOURCE
When it comes to chalkboard decals, **Wallies.com** has the best and largest variety of size options I've found—which is key if you plan to cover something as big as a refrigerator.

HOW-TO: CHALKBOARD FRIDGE

WHAT YOU NEED
- Screwdriver
- 3, 25- by 38-inch big chalkboard decals*
- X-ACTO knife

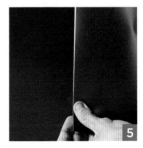

STEP 1
Remove your refrigerator and freezer door handles. They screw right off. In most cases there are only three screws for each door—two on the top, one on the bottom.

STEP 2
We'll start with your freezer door, which will need one decal. Peel the backing off the first 3 or 4 inches. Line up the sticky side with the inside edge of your freezer door—the corner closest to the rubber suction lining. Once straight, attach the decal to your door by smoothing down the surface with your palm.

STEP 3
Continue attaching your decal to the freezer door by peeling off 6-inch sections of backing at a time, and smoothing your way horizontally across the front. Run your palm side to side—not up and down, which causes more air bubbles.

STEP 4
When you've rounded the corner and reached the edge of the opposite side of your freezer door, use an X-ACTO knife to trim any excess decal along the top, bottom, and sides.

STEP 5
Repeat Steps 2 through 4 to attach your last two chalkboard decals to the front of your refrigerator door. You'll need to stack two, since this door is longer, so be sure to create a clean, straight line where the edges meet.

STEP 6
Reattach your refrigerator and freezer door handles—after giving them a quick rinse in warm, soapy water (who knows the last time they were properly cleaned!).

*Measurements are based on an average-size, two-door refrigerator.

GO FOR BOLD

Love the drama of a big, graphic pattern but not quite ready to make a commitment? These chalkboard decals are the perfect place to test the waters. Draw a chevron stripe that repeats on all of your cabinet fronts, or try polka dots that skip across the refrigerator. You can even map out a checkerboard effect. This is an easy way to do something really graphic in a room. So what if it takes you a little outside your comfort zone? Simply wipe down the decals with a wet rag, and you've got a clean slate to try something new.

DRESSING ROOM

We're all guilty of the trial-and-error try-on sessions that result in half our wardrobe being discarded in a pile on the bedroom floor. This is why absolutely everyone—guy or girl—needs a designated place to get dressed. Julie's dresser was originally at the opposite end of her bedroom, which regularly led to a trail of clothing slung from there to the closet. So I slid her dresser down the wall, closer to the closet door. When space allows, isolate everything you need to get dressed in one area of your room. If you can pull things out of the closet and dresser from the same spot, you're far more likely to put it back where it goes if you decide not to wear it. Julie was so surprised when this one move saved her a handful of precious minutes in the morning.

SMOKE & MIRRORS

The sliding closet doors in Julie's bedroom could have been stolen from a Vegas hotel back in the 1970s. They were framed in a thick, supershiny brass that felt completely out of place next to all the bright colors we were adding on the wall and bed. They needed a modern update. So with the permission of the landlord, I spray-painted them silver. Then I added graphic decals along the sides to break up the outdated wall-of-mirrors look (see page 149 for instructions on making your own decal mirror). The decals gave the room a much needed hit of pattern, while making the "dressing room" area a happier place to get ready.

A PERUVIAN PALETTE

Color was not something Julie was comfortable with. But the only way to bring her old-timey bed frame into the twenty-first century was through the use of bold, modern colors—and lots of them. So I chose an inspiration I knew Julie was already fond of: the bright raspberries and minty greens of a typical Peruvian blanket. After spending a year in this South American country, Julie was enamored with the culture. Integrating those shades into her bedroom brought on a sense of nostalgia—instead of color shock. Whenever you're on the fence about color, start with a palette inspired by something you love: a location, a restaurant, even the pattern of a dress.

DECAL MIRROR

HOW-TO: DECAL MIRROR

WHAT YOU NEED

- Drop cloth
- Scrap newspaper
- Painter's tape
- Matte gray spray paint
- 4, 24- by 48-inch decal sheets
- Ruler
- X-ACTO knife
- Measuring tape
- Pencil
- Scissors
- Glass cleaner

STEP 1

Remove your sliding doors from the track. Push up while angling the door toward you, and it should slip right out. Take your doors outside, and lay them on top of a drop cloth. (If an outdoor space isn't an option, just be sure you have a very large drop cloth to work on.)

STEP 2

Cover the mirror portion of your doors with scrap newspaper; then outline the trim with painter's tape. Be sure the mirror is securely covered because the spray paint will cause permanent speckles on the glass.

STEP 3

Spray paint the frame of your doors, keeping the nozzle about 12 inches away from the surface. Let it dry for twenty minutes; then apply a second coat, making sure to even out any drips or splatters. Let it dry completely, about one hour.

STEP 4

While your paint is drying, measure and cut your decal strips. Flip the decal over, and mark your measurements in pencil on the back. My 4 decals were all 2 feet wide, so I cut each in half lengthwise with an X-ACTO knife to get eight, 6-inch-wide strips to frame the four sides of my doors. (It will take two strips to cover each side, since most doors are 6 feet tall and these decals are 4 feet long.)

STEP 5

Check that your frame is good and dry, and remove all your painter's tape and newspaper. Use glass cleaner and wipe down your mirror to remove any leftover dirt and debris before applying the decals.

STEP 6

Peel the backing off the first 6 inches of a decal strip. Line it up with the side and top corner of your door. Use your palm to press the sticky side to the glass, smoothing in a downward motion—which causes fewer air bubbles. Work your way down the mirror in 6-inch increments, repeating this process, until you reach the bottom of your decal strip.

STEP 7

Line up the pattern of your next decal strip with the endpoint of your previous one. Use scissors and a straightedge to cut the decal at this point. Peel the backing off the first 6 inches, and follow the technique in Step 6 until you reach the bottom of your door. Trim the leftover decal with an X-ACTO knife. (Repeat Steps 6 and 7 on the remaining three sides of your 2 doors.)

STEP 8

Reattach your doors to their tracks by angling the castors back into the track and pulling down to lock them in place.

CHEAT SHEET:
THE SCHOLAR

1

NOT SURE WHAT YOUR STYLE REALLY IS? Use a favorite restaurant, bar, or travel destination as a jumping off point for inspiration.

2

BREAK UP THOSE MATCHING FURNITURE sets. They add nothing to the personality of a room.

3

HIDE SHODDY CABINETRY with removable decals. They draw attention to the good details, while covering the bad.

4

GIVE A BRICK WALL—or even a plain one—even more character by making your own exposed beams with store-bought wood planks.

5

DON'T SWEAT THE BIG STUFF, but spend some time on the little things. A sofa won't add nearly as much personality as an armload of throw pillows or artwork on the walls.

THE REBEL

WHO: Joe

JOB: Graphic designer

LIVES IN: Capitol Hill, Seattle

MEASUREMENTS: 300 square feet

JOE RELOCATED TO SEATTLE FROM DENVER FASTER THAN THE INK COULD DRY ON HIS COLLEGE DIPLOMA.

The street culture, the skate community, and all the graffiti art projects were a huge inspiration for his own graphic design work. His first lesson, however, was that square footage in this port city comes at a premium. He couldn't afford anything more than a studio on his hourly wage. Plus, he needed to live within walking distance to his new job at a skatewear brand in Capitol Hill. This meant his apartment hunting was restricted to a ten-block radius in a neighborhood home to some of the oldest, most desirable buildings in the city—and some of the shadiest.

After two months of subletting with four other Craigslisters, Joe found a 300-square-foot studio located four blocks from his office. The third-floor walk-up had no bells and whistles and barely enough space to fit Joe's necessities—a desk, sofa, and full-size bed. But as it turns out, the small size suited Joe's simplified lifestyle, which was centered on the philosophy that you should own what you need, nothing more. I support this in theory, but when I walked into Joe's apartment it looked like an Ikea display room. Joe is a graphic designer, a skater, and a collector of typography, and his apartment was white walls and a hodgepodge of pale furniture. It was missing life. So I was there to perform some design CPR—not by adding new things but by revamping a lot of what he already owned.

MAKING WAVES

>> **SECRET SOURCE**
This striped slipcover is from **Bemz.com**, a Swedish company that makes slipcovers specially cut for Ikea sofas and chairs. There are dozens of colors and fabrics—including prints by big design houses like Marimekko and Designers Guild. It's a cost-efficient way to breathe new life into an old sofa (especially one that survived college with you).

Natural light spilled into Joe's main room for the better part of the day thanks to the big double windows. I loved how the white walls and blinds heightened that effect, but I didn't want to leave everything completely white because, well, it felt too boring. So I decided to do this cool faded-paint effect along the base of the wall (see page 171 for instructions), and echoed it on the curtain panels (see page 161 for instructions).

Joe spends a lot of his post-work hours hanging out along Seattle's waterfront. On a clear day, you can make out a speck of blue horizon in the distance from his window. To bring a bit of that inspiration closer to home, I chose a watery blue paint shade, which ended up looking like waves receding on a beach once it was on the wall. And as a bonus, dividing the wall with a dark paint color on the bottom made the ceilings feel higher. By keeping all the furniture below this halfway mark, the room instantly seemed more open and bright.

THE FLOOR PLAN

Joe had a small list of "musts" for his apartment, one of which was that the main room have a sofa, bed, and desk. The thought of using the fold-out kitchen table as a workspace and the bed as a sofa made him a little nuts. But the problem was . . . how to fit three large pieces of furniture in a 10- by 12-foot room with only a single unobstructed wall? The solution: furniture placement that goes against the norm. Typically, you wouldn't put a sofa in front of a window because it blocks light, but Joe's slid neatly under the ledge of the windowsill. And in most instances you'd place the long side of a desk and the short side of a bed against the wall, but we reversed those. Don't be afraid to puzzle-piece things together: doing the opposite of what's expected might be the only way to make everything fit.

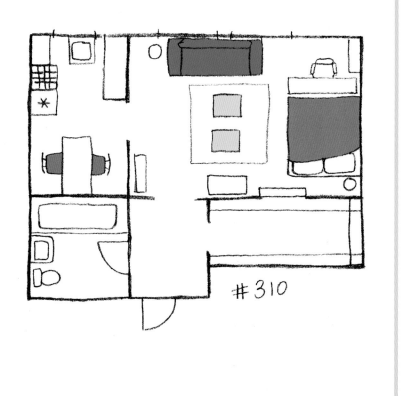

#310

PLUMBING
WITH A VIEW,
P. 168

DIP-DYE
CURTAINS,
P. 161

FADED
PAINT,
P. 171

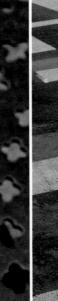

OUTSIDE IN

Here's the thing about Seattle: it's gritty, especially around Joe's apartment. You can't go a single block without passing a wall plastered with layers of shredded posters and fliers. More often than not, the sidewalk is being used as someone's blank canvas—with or without permission from the law. And everything is dusted with just the thinnest layer of rust. Pristine and perfect don't exist on the streets of Joe's new city—and he didn't want them to exist in his apartment either.

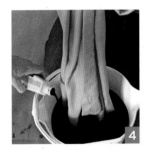

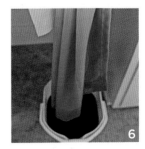

HOW-TO: DIP-DYE CURTAINS

WHAT YOU NEED

- Drop cloth
- 8-ounce bottle of liquid fabric dye
- 4-gallon bucket (or larger)
- Dish washing gloves
- Curtains*

STEP 1

Cover your work area with a drop cloth. Mix half the bottle of liquid fabric dye with 3 gallons of warm water in your bucket and stir.

STEP 2

Run your curtains under warm water, and

TIP: If you're going to match this effect on the wall, the way we did, dye your curtains first. It's far easier to match the height of the faded paint on your walls to the height of the dye on your curtains than vice versa.

wring them out. You want them damp, not dripping wet when you start.

STEP 3

Submerge half your curtain in the bucket, and let it sit for five minutes. (I like to wear a dish washing glove on the hand that will be touching the dyed end of the curtain and leave my other hand bare—so there's less chance of getting dye where it doesn't belong.)

STEP 4

Pull one-third of the submerged curtain out of the bucket—so you're left with two-thirds still in the dye. Don't worry about your measurements being exact.

STEP 5

Add half of the dye left in your bottle to the water, making sure not to pour it directly onto the submerged fabric. Mix the dye with the water by carefully swirling it around with your gloved hand. Let sit for five minutes.

STEP 6

Pull another third of the submerged curtain out of the bucket, so

only one-third is left in the dye.

STEP 7

Add the rest of the dye left in your bottle to the water—following the same directions from Step 5—and let sit for five minutes.

STEP 8

Remove the rest of the curtain from your bucket, and hang it straight to dry over your drop cloth.

*Opt for curtains in a sturdy fabric like cotton or linen. This dip-dye process is not recommended for polyester, acrylic, or fabrics with a rubber backing.

> "REMEMBER, NOTHING IS PERMANENT. IF YOU HANG SOMETHING ON THE WALL YOU DON'T LIKE A WEEK LATER, TAKE IT DOWN."

I'D LIKE TO BUY A VOWEL, PLEASE

Joe collects typography books, something you'd never know by looking at his apartment—unless you took the time to sift through the numerous piles on his floor. There was no artwork, let alone a pattern of any kind, in the entire space. I've met a lot of people like Joe, who have a hard time committing to the small details, like throw pillows or what to hang on the wall. It can feel overwhelming, since these are the items that are supposed to reflect "you" the most. But remember, nothing is permanent. If you hang something on the wall you don't like a week later, take it down. Trying something you end up not loving is far better than doing nothing at all.

In Joe's apartment, I bought three graphic throw pillows from a local thrift store and mixed them in with the solid black ones he already owned. He can swap them back and forth between the sofa and bed to change the mood of the whole room. Then, to showcase his love of typography, I spray-painted one of his favorite mottos—"I Am Who I Am"—across three canvases using letter stencils from Home Depot. It had the street-art feel Joe loves and brought a unique, personal touch to the space.

TABLE FOR TWO

Among Joe's haul from Ikea were two really basic coffee tables in a faux-natural wood finish. They were small and easy to move around, so Joe could use them for just about anything. To increase the mobility, I wanted to update them with cool industrial wheels. But before starting, I covered the faux-wood finish with a sleek, glossy black paint. When buying furniture from mass market stores like Ikea or Target, always opt for a streamlined piece in solid black. It will look like it could have come from any number of expensive boutiques.

5 MINUTE UPDATE: WHEELIE COFFEE TABLE

WHAT YOU NEED: 4 swivel-base caster wheels • 1 Sharpie • ⅟₁₆-inch drill bit • Electric drill • Screwdriver

STEP 1: Turn your table over. Line up your caster wheels in the center of each leg. Mark the points where you need to drill with a Sharpie. **STEP 2:** Using a ⅟₁₆-inch drill bit, drill a hole at each mark. (Drill slowly so you don't split the wood.) **STEP 3:** Line up your caster holes with the holes you just drilled and attach your caster base with the screws provided. Then flip your table back over, and you're off and rolling.

WALK-THRU CLOSET

Most first apartments have that one weird quirk that makes no sense. In Joe's apartment, that quirk was a decent-size walk-in closet with two doorways—one off the entryway and one off the main room. The double entries cut the functionality of his only storage space in half. His solution was to hang a sheet in each doorframe in the hopes of hiding the stashed-away chaos inside. But what he really needed was a solid wall and a single doorway to maximize the usage, so I came up with a way to remedy the problem: turn the doorway in the main room into a bookcase.

The project is simple (see page 167 for instructions on building your own doorway bookcase), and gave Joe the luxury of shelves big enough to store those books he'd been piling up. Plus, it created another uninterrupted wall in the main room, which changed the traffic flow and let us have a bit more space to play around with furniture placement—like the bed and desk. You can do this in most any doorway, and the best part is that you're actually able to personalize the shelf placement and height to fit your needs: books, records, artwork, a stereo, and so on.

ORANGE BURST

Between the white walls and strategic hits of blues, blacks, and grays, Joe's apartment felt somewhat expectedly masculine. I wanted to toss in a "surprise" element—to keep him on his toes—so I selected a color that was completely opposite to the cool tones I'd already introduced . . . orange. Yep, it's a pretty tricky color. But the key is finding a shade with enough red undertones to keep it from feeling too young. I used it on the bookcase, in the bathroom, and in the kitchen, so no matter where you were standing in the apartment you got a shot of the bright, happy hue.

TIP: Stack books on their sides and then shelve them. It increases the surface area you have to create displays, while also giving you a range of heights to work with. Plus, it's the perfect solution for bookcases without sides.

>> SECRET SOURCE

Skurniture.com is a West Coast brand that creates furniture legs in various finishes to turn skate decks into cool tables. I did this with one of Joe's old skateboards, so he would have a small catchall table in the main room—and then I used the wheels as bookends.

HOW-TO: DOORWAY BOOKCASE

WHAT YOU NEED

- 1 gallon of semigloss paint
- 1, 2-inch-wide paint brush
- 1 paint roller
- 1 standard sheet of 4- by 8-foot plywood*
- 4 pieces of 10- by 30-inch lumber (for shelves)
- Electric drill
- 10, 1-inch wood screws
- 8 shelf brackets
- 16, 1/4-inch wood screws
- Screwdriver
- Level
- Sharpie
- 1/8-inch drill bit
- 16, 1-inch bolts with corresponding nuts and washers
- Pliers

STEP 1

Paint the four shelves—edges and all—and one side of your sheet of plywood. It may take extra coats to evenly cover your plywood because the wood is so porous. Let dry completely, about three hours for each coat.

STEP 2

Attach your sheet of plywood to the backside of your door frame—here, that was the closet side—using your electric drill and 1-inch wood screws. Screw your plywood directly into the door frame, starting with each of the four corners. Then place a screw every foot or so around the frame.

STEP 3

Attach your brackets to your shelves using your screwdriver and 1/4-inch screws. Screw the bracket directly into the wood, making sure that whatever type of bracket you choose, your placement is consistent for each shelf.

STEP 4

Determine shelf placement on your sheet of plywood by using your level and bracketed shelves. Once everything is lined up to your liking, use your Sharpie to mark the places you will need to connect the brackets to the plywood. Then drill a hole at each mark with your electric drill and 1/8-inch drill bit.

STEP 5

Attach each shelf to your sheet of plywood by lining up your brackets with the holes you just drilled. Slip one of your 1-inch bolts through the hole—so the end is poking out the opposite side of the sheet of plywood (that is, the hidden side)—and tighten a nut and washer to the end with your pliers. Once all the shelves are firmly attached, start loading them up.

*Based on a standard 80- by 36-inch door frame.

CORNER OFFICE

Joe had a chair for his desk, a lamp for his desk, even an old-school gym clock to hang on the wall by his desk. However, when I first arrived, he did not have an actual desk. Nothing he found was cheap enough—and he still wasn't even sure a desk would fit in his apartment at that point.

During his hunt, Joe avoided the most obvious place, the no-name "clearance furniture closeout" store on his block. They exist in every city and can be intimidating for sure, but they are some of the best spots to find a deal—especially if you're looking for something really basic. That's where I found this desk for $75. The shape was straightforward: solid sides and one small drawer in the center. But once I painted the desk the same glossy black as the side tables and slid it against the bed, it gave the whole unit a built-in effect. So it no longer felt like the mattress was floating aimlessly on the wall—and the small corner was now firmly established as his workspace.

PLUMBING WITH A VIEW

The windows in Joe's main room were not a standard size, which made it impossible to find a curtain rod. Instead of paying a small fortune to have one custom-made, I headed to the plumbing aisle at the local Home Depot. You can have a pipe cut to any measurement you like, and it will work just as well as a normal curtain rod (if not better, since it's extra sturdy). I bought a half-inch pipe—you don't want anything bigger because it gets hard to fit your curtain over it—at the exact length needed, and all the wall-mountable connectors (three floor flanges, two elbow connectors, and one T connector) for about $50. I hung the curtains higher than the window frame—almost to the ceiling—which created the illusion of height and gave Joe the loft-like industrial feel he really wanted but thought he couldn't afford.

OPPOSITE: The subtle stripe on the lampshade was introduced to balance the wildness of the brushstrokes on the wall. It gave the desk an ever-so-slightly more polished finish.

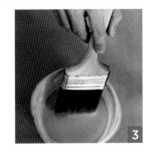

HOW-TO: FADED PAINT

WHAT YOU NEED

- Drop cloth
- 2, 2-inch-wide paint brushes
- 1 gallon of flat paint
- Painter's tape (optional)
- 1 paint roller
- 1 plastic container full of water

....

STEP 1

Cover your workspace with a drop cloth. Using one of your 2-inch paint brushes, outline the trim at the base of your wall. Depending on how steady you are with a paint brush, you may want to tape off the baseboard first.

STEP 2

Paint a 30-inch block across the bottom of the wall with your roller. Your measurements don't need to be perfect; you just want a solid bottom portion to work with.

STEP 3

Take the same 2-inch paint brush you used for the trim, and dip the end in your plastic container filled with water. You want it to be damp, but not so wet it's dripping.

STEP 4

Run the brush up the wall, so you're essentially stretching the paint that's already on the wall to create fade marks. There's no

right or wrong here; just play around until you find the height and frequency you like.

STEP 5

Using your other 2-inch paint brush, which should be dry, go back over the faded area to add extra wisps of texture—and to clean up any drip marks. Let the paint dry for two hours.

KITCHEN ALLEY

Apart from defrosting the occasional frozen pizza, Joe never cooks. He's more of a takeout kinda guy, which means his little alleyway of a kitchen was valuable square footage being wasted. There was no chance of my piquing Joe's interest in the culinary arts, but I did want to make this room a bit more habitable. It had great old details, including a built-in, café-style table that folded down when not in use. Joe was originally keeping the table down and storing his bike in that space. But once we remedied the situation with his closet, there was enough space for him to keep his bike there instead—finally making his table accessible.

When you're living with such minimal room, it's important to feel like you have a lot of different areas at your disposal—it keeps the claustrophobia at bay. So I painted all the walls the same semigloss orange I used on the doorway bookcase—and even trimmed the side of the table in this color—to really wake up the space and highlight the older architectural elements. Then I added some vintage glass jars from a local thrift store to introduce a typographic element to the kitchen. The end result was a bright, happy place for Joe to sit and enjoy his morning coffee—and perhaps a meal every now and again.

The kitchen cabinets were abnormally close to the counter, which meant all appliances—even the coffeemaker—had to be put away. I left the plates and coffee mugs out in order to make room in the cabinets for everything else.

A CHIP OFF THE OL' PAINT BLOCK

It's easy to chalk up a bathroom as a purely functional space that doesn't need any décor fanfare—which is exactly what Joe had done. Apart from a shower liner, a toothbrush, and a bar of soap, you'd never know anyone even lived here. But here's the problem with that: leaving a bathroom all white will show dirt and grime faster. Joe was by no means a "messy" guy, but by adding design elements to the room, we gave the eye something to focus on other than toothpaste residue in the sink. I used the last of my semigloss orange paint in here, then installed a little shelf for odds and ends, like washcloths and a toothbrush holder. But by far my favorite addition was the paint chip artwork. It was a fun, ten-minute project that brought the whole room together.

PAINT CHIP ARTWORK

STEP 1: Take any size blank canvas and line up an assortment of paint chips across the surface.

STEP 2: Use strips of black electrical tape between your paint chip squares to create a grid-like effect, while adhering the chips to the canvas. (Don't worry about lining up your paint chips perfectly; the electrical tape will make everything look nice and straight.)

HOW-TO: TILE TATTOOS

The white bathroom tiles wrapped around the room. I wanted to break that up by adding one of my favorite new inventions to the shower: Tile Tattoos. These are graphic squares that are easy to put on—and even easier to remove: you simply peel from a corner, and the whole thing comes off. I chose a sunburst in a rusty orange and placed them across a single row of tiles for a retro, Zen-like effect.

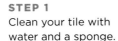

WHAT YOU NEED
- Tile Tattoos
- Sponge
- Credit card

STEP 1
Clean your tile with water and a sponge.

STEP 2
Wet the back of your Tile Tattoo with water. There should be minimal drops.

STEP 3
Press the wet side of the Tile Tattoo to the tile. Since both surfaces are damp, they should cling together but still have a little slide to them.

STEP 4
Firmly press your Tile Tattoo to the tile, and use the side of a credit card to squeegee all the water out from between the two, making sure the tile stays straight. Once all the water and air bubbles are gone, the Tile Tattoo is set.

CHEAT SHEET:
THE REBEL

1

IN SMALL ROOMS, paint a darker color on the bottom half of your wall. It anchors the space, while making it feel bright and airy.

2

IT'S THE UNUSUAL TOUCHES that add the most personality, so use your imagination— a skateboard table, a mailbox desk sorter, even plumbing pipes as curtain rods.

3

TAKE CONTROL OF YOUR FLOOR PLAN. If something doesn't make sense for you, like two doorways into a single closet, think of ways to make the space fit your lifestyle— not vice versa.

4

STUDIO LIVING MEANS GETTING CREATIVE with your furniture arrangements. Don't just line your wall with furniture. Instead, try to angle pieces to create specific areas: a place to sit, a place to work, a place to sleep, and so on.

5

ART IS EVERYWHERE— cheap stencils, free paint chips—look around and take advantage. There are plenty of ways to express yourself for hardly any money.

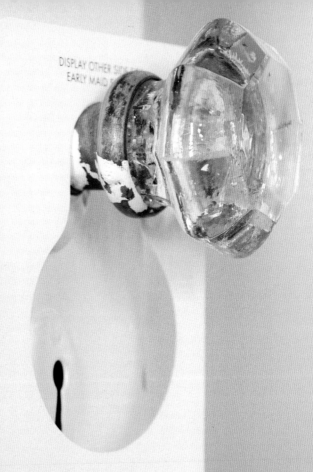

DISPLAY OTHER SIDE
EARLY MAID

PLEASE

DO NOT
DISTURB

THE HOMEBODY

WHO: Kyle

JOB: Interior designer

LIVES IN: Miracle Mile, LA

MEASUREMENTS:
700 square feet

COME ON IN! WELCOME TO MY HOME AND OFFICE— THE PLACE YOU CAN FIND ME 99 PERCENT OF THE TIME.

I sleep here, work here, and entertain here (and "here" is only 700 square feet). It's small, but when I moved into this Craftsman-style one-bedroom two years ago, it was the most space I'd been able to call my own, well, ever.

I had big ideas for an apartment with tiny rooms and lots of architectural quirks to contend with: rounded door frames, low-sitting windows, a nonworking heating system that spanned the height of one living room wall. I wanted to have dinner parties for eight, a waiting area for clients, and a game table for Scrabble marathons. But just like everyone else, I had to give my over-the-top vision a stern reality check. Not only was there no room to do any of this on the grand scale I'd imagined but there was also no budget. What little money I had to spend was allotted to functional things, like a place to sit down and possibly silverware.

That doesn't mean I gave up on the things I wanted though. I focused on slowly collecting furniture I really loved that could do double-duty: ottomans that would break down into transitional seating for client visits and a media console that would work as an appetizer buffet when I have parties. Getting my apartment to the point you see it in this chapter has been a two-year labor of love—and a tough lesson in patience.

SEATING FOR NINE, PLEASE

Seating was at the top of my priority list. I love playing host, but my client meetings require enough surface area to spread out fabric swatches, floor plans, and such. So I needed seating that would work as an extra tabletop when necessary. I lined the wall beneath my windows with two leather benches—scored at a Crate&Barrel floor sample sale—that could be pulled up to the coffee table. Then I added a vinyl pouf next to the sofa, since there was no room left for a proper chair. By keeping the pieces my guests could sit on small, I was able to double the number of people that could sit comfortably in my 10- by 15-foot room. So my rule is this: don't get caught up in the necessity of having a chair or even a sofa in your living room. Benches, poufs, crates covered in pillows, or even a slip-covered twin mattress can work just as well.

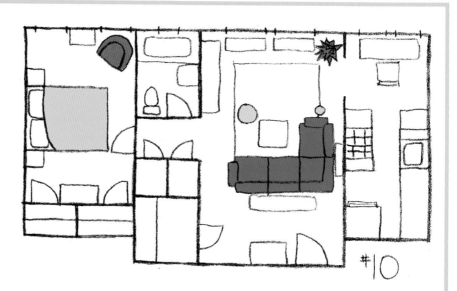

THE FLOOR PLAN

Since my apartment has so many different functions, figuring out a floor plan meant first allocating certain areas for certain tasks. My living room is where I meet with clients, host game nights, and, of course, relax in front of the television. The small dining room became my office. And my bedroom is also a pseudo-library for my books and vast *Architectural Digest* collection. (Confession: I've been a subscriber since I was thirteen years old.) The lesson: knowing how a space will be used makes filling it a much more focused undertaking.

ROOM WITHOUT A VIEW

To play off the warm, taupey brown shade of the walls, I chose blinds in a dark wood tone, which cast a beautiful, moody light. The big blue skies and sun-filled days were a huge part of what drew me to LA from my hometown of Chicago. The truth of my situation is this, though: my apartment building is a mere 3 feet from another apartment building. With the blinds up, I enjoy a view of my neighbor's kitchen window and a lot of deteriorated baby blue wall. But I always say, fake what you don't have. The alleyway between the two buildings gets plenty of sun exposure, so I outfitted each of my windows with these blinds that have slightly oversized panels. The panels let in the perfect amount of soft light and still allow for plenty of privacy—without making me feel closed in.

A TEXTURAL MEDLEY

There are two ways to add depth to a room: layer patterns (see page 64 for tips) or layer texture. Since my goal was a calm, masculine, woodsy aesthetic—and not something dramatic—I did the latter. My whole apartment is a palette of earthy browns with the occasional pop of red or orange. Without texture, it would be flat, neutral, and boring. But whereas the color scheme is safe, the textural elements in the living room alone have upped the ante tenfold. Fuzzy pillows sit on sleek leather benches. My coffee table and side table are made from tree stumps. The pendant floor lamp is metal. The herringbone rug is jute. The throw pillows are cableknit. The wallpapered piece of wood behind the sofa, which is actually covering a hideous heater (see page 187 for making your own wallpapered heater cover), is meant to look like tree bark. Even the walls are textured. By sticking with a simple palette, I could go wild with different materials and finishes and not worry about it feeling like too much. The result: a warm, texturally diverse room with tons of interesting details.

A QUICK NOTE ON COFFEE TABLES

They're among the smallest pieces of furniture you own but the easiest to get wrong. It only takes a few inches to throw off the delicate balance between your sofa and coffee table. Here are a few rules to help you avoid some common pitfalls:

- The height of your coffee table should be equal to or less than the height of the seat on your sofa.

- If you have a sectional like mine, the coffee table should nestle into the nook created by the sofa's L shape.

- You should leave enough room between the edge of the coffee table and the edge of the sofa for someone to walk through, so no less than a foot.

WALLPAPERED HEATER COVER

- WALLPAPER ROLL
- PAINT TRAY
- PAINT ROLLER
- WALLPAPER PASTE
- CORNER BRACKETS
- SCREW DRIVER
- SPONGE

HOW-TO: WALLPAPERED HEATER COVER*

WHAT YOU NEED

- 4- by 8-foot sheet of plywood
- 10 L-shaped corner bracket kits (with screws)
- Screwdriver
- Paste-the-Wall wallpaper (it's removable!)
- X-ACTO knife
- Sponge
- 1 container wallpaper paste
- Paint tray
- Thick paint roller
- Plastic putty knife

STEP 1

Measure the depth of your heater. Add 1 inch, and then have your local hardware store cut that amount from each of the long sides of your sheet of plywood. Be sure to double-check that the width of the center piece after you cut is wider than the width of your heater.

STEP 2

Lay your plywood pieces on the ground, as if they were still one sheet. Flip the two sides up, so their width is perpendicular to the floor. Stack them on top of the outer edges of

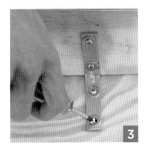

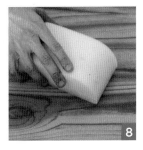

your middle piece—so the edges are flush. (You should have a squared-off U shape.)

STEP 3

Using your L-shaped corner bracket kits—five on each side—connect the two sides to your middle piece. Be sure to use a bracket at the top and bottom of each side, and then space out the remaining three brackets evenly over the rest of the length of your plywood.

STEP 4

Flip over your plywood box. Now, you're ready to precut your wallpaper strips. Start at the edge of one of your corner pieces, and roll out your wallpaper to cover the entire length. Leave 1 to 2 inches to spare at the top and bottom of your plywood box; then cut your first wallpaper strip using your X-ACTO knife. Measure and cut the rest of your wallpaper strips based on this length, making sure your pattern lines up along the way.

STEP 5

Wipe the plywood box with a damp sponge to get rid of any debris. If

there are large knots, you will need to fill them with wood putty (see page 188 for instructions). Pour your wallpaper paste into the paint tray. Then, using your paint roller, generously cover the entire surface of your plywood box. It should look like the consistency of skim milk.

STEP 6

Lay your first wallpaper strip on the plywood box, making sure to create a clean fold along the corner. Using a plastic putty knife, gently smooth any lines or bubbles under the paper. Continue papering across the entirety of your plywood box, again, making sure your patterns are lining up.

STEP 7

Using your X-ACTO knife, trim any excess

wallpaper from the top and bottom of your plywood box.

STEP 8

Take a damp sponge and wipe off any excess wallpaper paste. Let the cover sit for at least two hours before placing it over your heater. It should stay put just fine, but for extra support, you can use two more L-shaped corner brackets and adhere the cover directly to your wall.

*This project is meant for covering heaters not currently in use. Do not cover a unit you need access to.

TIP: Home Depot gives you two free cuts when you buy a full sheet of lumber. So if you have your measurements, you can leave with your pieces ready to assemble.

WHO'S AFRAID OF A LITTLE WHITE BOX?

As an interior designer, walking into an empty apartment of nothing but white walls and wooden floors is pure bliss. (Oh, the possibilities!) But to most everyone else, that same white box is as intimidating as a middle school bully—sitting there in all its pristine blankness waiting to mock you after one wrong paint selection. But here's the thing: decorating should feel more like a date than a wedding—nothing is actually long term. So when faced with four white walls, simply pick an inspiring starting point and build from there. For me, that was this sunburst mirror. It was my first "adult" decorating splurge, and I knew I wanted it to be a focal point in the room—which is how I landed on painting my walls brown. (It highlights the mirror's golden tones perfectly.) But I must have tried close to a dozen shades before finally landing on this taupey shade. The moral of this story: don't be afraid to make mistakes.

HOW-TO: REPAIRING CHIPPED WOOD FURNITURE

WHAT YOU NEED

- 1 container of stainable wood putty
- Putty knife
- 1 sheet of fine-grit sandpaper
- Damp rag
- Wood stain marker

STEP 1
Using your putty knife, fill the chipped area with wood putty. Don't worry about smooth edges or overfilling; you'll sand everything to fit later. Let dry for one hour.

STEP 2
Once your wood putty is firm, take the fine-grit sandpaper and sand the puttied area until the surface is flush with the rest of your piece. Note: When dealing with corners, be sure to keep the edges nice and sharp. Sand both sides using an up-and-down motion until you have an even corner.

STEP 3
Wipe the puttied area with a damp rag to clean off as much of the sanded particles as possible. Then, using the stain marker, which should match the stain on whatever you're filling in, color over the puttied area. It only takes one coat, but let it dry for thirty minutes before touching it.

THE WAITING GAME

Even though a desk was at the top of my furniture wish list, it took me nearly nine months to find the right one. I was pretty insistent that my desk face out a window. Anyone who works from home will agree, it's the only way to keep from getting distracted by household chores or worse yet, the television. But the windows in my apartment sit a tad lower than normal, so I needed to find a desk that would slide under the windowsill and not jut out farther than the archway door that connected the kitchen to the living room—which proved to be pretty difficult. After months of hunching over my laptop at the coffee table, I found this small scale industrial metal tanker desk on Craigslist. It was exactly the classic style I wanted, only shrunken down. The moral of this story: you really can find the needle in the haystack—just keep digging!

REDEFINING ROOMS

Never take a room at face value. Reassess your space and turn it into what you really need. I needed an office more than a dining room, so that's what this little nook off my kitchen became.

> " **I'D CHOOSE** LESS LIVING SPACE **IN FAVOR OF** MORE STORAGE ANY DAY."

STORAGE VS. SPACE—A CONUNDRUM

When I was apartment hunting, I had the option of looking at another rental in my building that was a whole 50 square feet larger and listed at the exact same price. The difference: storage. My apartment has a big closet off the living room, which is packed to capacity with my bicycle, set props, and samples. I'd choose less living space in favor of more storage any day. It makes such a difference when you have a proper place to put things away.

Along those same lines, I discovered the drawers of my new desk weren't nearly enough storage for all the little odds and ends my job requires. Since I had other plans for my dishes (see page 193 for details), I decided to turn the counter-height, glass-front cabinets that separated the kitchen from my little office into extra storage. I bought a bunch of dark wood boxes from the Container Store for about $8 each, printed out circular labels for them, and threw everything from paintbrushes to molding samples inside before stashing them away in the cabinets. Most apartments have more storage than you think, so look for underutilized spaces and put them to use.

THE CHEF IS IN

Like most older LA apartments, mine had a pretty rundown kitchen. There was only one wall cabinet, minimal counters, and a whole lot of dead space on the walls. Nothing was what you'd call particularly functional, especially for someone who enjoys cooking. So I took a few notes from the industrial-style kitchens you'd find at most restaurants and headed down to my local restaurant supply store. These places are truly genius: they cut out the intermediate dealers, so everything is a quarter the price you'd normally pay. Plus, they have everything you could ever need—and more.

The single wall cabinet unit in my kitchen had to hold all my food, which meant everything else—pots, pans, plates, glasses, and such—would need to be out in the open. I decided to hang all my cookware from the wall behind my stove using a chicken wire fixture I built myself (see page 195 for instructions on making your own chicken wire pot rack). Then I grabbed two industrial-strength metal shelves to stack my dishes and glasses on. Remember, dishes can get pretty heavy, so you need something reinforced and sturdy. A simple floating shelf won't work. In the end, I couldn't have been happier with my little alleyway-of-a-kitchen that left everything out in the open.

TIP: If your glassware, like mine, tends to disappear as if it were disposable, stock up on white or black dishes and clear glasses. Apart from flowing color-wise, these basics are so much easier to replace when they inevitably go missing.

OPPOSITE: A collection of canisters help keep my counter clutter-free. I use them to hold sugar, flour, and all my favorite spices.

HOW-TO: CHICKEN WIRE POT RACK

WHAT YOU NEED

- Measuring tape
- Pencil
- 1 roll, $1/2$-inch chicken wire
- Tin snips
- Power drill
- $5/16$-inch drill bit
- 6 heavy-duty anchors
- 24, $1/4$-inch washers
- 6 heavy-duty screws (at least 2 inches)
- S hooks (equal to the number of pots you want to hang)

STEP 1

With your pencil, measure and mark the space on your wall that you want to use for your pot rack. Cut your chicken wire to fit using tin snips.

STEP 2

Along your two sides, measure and mark the halfway point between your top and bottom corners. Drill a hole in the wall at these two marks and at each of your four corners—for six holes total—and insert your anchors.

STEP 3

You need to create room between the wall and your chicken wire so that you can hang things without scratching the wall paint. To start, stack 4 washers together, and place them under one of the corner squares in your chicken wire. Then place 2 more washers on top. (You're creating a sandwich effect on either side of the opening in your chicken wire.) Slide one screw through the center of your stack, and screw it into the wall anchor. (So coming away from the wall, the lineup should be: wall anchor + 4 washers + chicken wire + 2 washers + screw head.)

STEP 4

Repeat Step 3 at each of your remaining 5 marked anchors, making sure your chicken wire is taut as you work your way around the perimeter.

STEP 5

Start hanging! String your S hooks through the holes in your pot handles and onto a square on your grid. Avoid hanging anything as heavy as cast iron, but everything else—including pasta spoons, strainers, even your coffee mugs—should work just fine.

THE DIGNIFIED OUTDOORSMAN

Don't get me wrong: I love a serene bedroom as much as the next person. But whenever I design a bedroom for myself, I like it to be a little more playful—maybe it's because I had to share a room with my sister growing up. I have to have an element of boyhood fun in my space. So instead of keeping the masculine, woodsy aesthetic streamlined and sophisticated—as I'd done throughout the rest of my apartment—I really gave the bedroom a tongue-in-cheek twist on the theme. I topped my striped bedding with an old-school English coat of arms throw pillow (a gift from my mom), and I mounted a cardboard stag head above my bed—equipped with a dapper tie. I like to think the room has a Robin Hood quality to it—if Robin Hood lived in modern-day LA, that is.

HOW-TO: PAINT A PERFECT CIRCLE

Since earthquakes are a real concern on the West Coast, I was scared to put anything heavier than this cardboard stag on the wall above my headboard. But on its own, it didn't take up enough room to feel substantial. So I decided to paint a circle around it in the hopes of getting the effect of an actual mount.

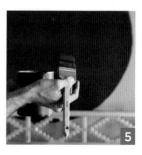

WHAT YOU NEED
- Measuring tape
- 1 metal tack
- String
- Pencil
- 2-inch-wide paint brush
- Paint

STEP 1
Determine the diameter of your circle, and push your metal tack into the center point of that measurement. For instance, I wanted my circle to be 24 inches in diameter, so I placed my tack at the 12-inch mark.

STEP 2
Tie one end of your string to the tack. From there, measure half the distance of your diameter on your piece of string—again, that was 12 inches here. Add 1 inch to that measurement, and cut your string. Use the extra inch to tie the other end of your string to your pencil—making sure the length of the string between the pencil and nail is still half the length of your diameter.

STEP 3
Take your pencil and trace a circle around the tack. Keep the string taut while drawing.

STEP 4
Ta-da! You have your circle. Now, using your 2-inch paint brush, trace the outer edge of your circle with paint, creating a frame.

STEP 5
Paint the center of your circle. (You want to outline first because it will lessen the chances of paint drips later.)

LOVINGLY COLLECTED

My bedroom was piecemealed together with a lot of imagination and two years of relentless thrift store visits. I found the bed frame in a junk store in LA's Echo Park neighborhood and the bedside tables almost a year later at the same place. The dresser is from a thrift store in nearby Silverlake, and my ever-growing collection of white vases has been culled from the many design jobs I've had over the years. I have a serious aversion to matching sets, especially when it comes to furniture—there's something so predictable about them—but you still want everything to feel cohesive, even if there are slightly different shades of wood stain or a century's worth of separate design eras that need to coexist. My Southwestern-style bed frame, for instance, was a rusty shade of white when I found it. The bedside tables have an art deco feel. And the dresser is a midcentury modern piece that originally had bronze handles.

Clearly, there were a lot of different vibes happening here. But just as I did with my mismatched assortment of vases, I used color—well technically, matching hardware—to create a thread of similarity throughout all the furniture. It's a little known fact, but most thrift stores—and all furniture restoration shops—don't charge much to spray paint something. I had the bed frame and all of the handles from the dresser and bedside tables spray painted the same metallic shade of silver. This one small step made a ramshackle assortment feel like a cohesive—but not too matchy—mix.

RAWHIDE

Whenever I buy a rug for a bedroom, I have an inner battle with myself. On the one hand, you want something soft to step on first thing in the morning. But on the other, rugs large enough to fit under a bed are never cheap. You end up paying a lot for something you only use a little of. This is why cowhide rugs are so perfect for the bedroom: the shape is organic, so there's no right or wrong in terms of where it stops or begins. You can have it under the bottom half of your bed or just under a single side. It will always feel well proportioned.

CHEAT SHEET:
THE HOMEBODY

1

LAYERING TEXTURES is a sophisticated way to add depth to a room.

2

DON'T LET THAT EMPTY WALL SPACE in your tiny kitchen go to waste. Cabinets or not, you can turn it into storage.

3

REDEFINE THE ROOMS IN YOUR APARTMENT. It should fit your lifestyle, not what the broker claims it should be.

4

EVERY PROBLEM, including built-in eyesores, has a creative solution.

5

MIX AND MATCH YOUR FURNITURE. Don't ever—ever—get trapped into a set.

THE BOHEMIAN

WHO: Adrian

JOB: Real estate agent

LIVES IN: Inman Park, Atlanta

MEASUREMENTS: 500 square feet

ATLANTA IS ONE OF THOSE SPRAWLING CITIES MADE UP OF DISTINCT LITTLE NEIGHBORHOODS RATHER THAN A DOMINANT BUSTLING DOWNTOWN.

No matter where you work, a commute is a given. So when Adrian began her apartment search—her first sans roommates—picking the right neighborhood topped her list of priorities. She wanted a safe, renter-friendly, artsy community that wasn't a bunch of identical cement block buildings. Add to that her budget cap of $700 per month, and it felt like a rather tall order—even for a real estate agent. She had her heart set on living in the historic Little Five Points area when, through a friend of a friend, she found this attic apartment in a restored 1920s Victorian home located in Inman Park—a neighboring community. It took all of five minutes in the cozy space to reignite Adrian's childhood infatuation with treehouses—and a mere five minutes more for the rental agreement to be signed.

Adrian has an adventurous, fly-by-the-seat-of-her-pants approach to life. When she has a whim, she usually follows it—and that's exactly how she ended up in this charming, brightly lit apartment that did not have a single uninterrupted, full-size wall and angled ceilings that allowed her to fully stand up in only one-third of the space. Personality-wise it couldn't have been cooler; logistically, though, it was a bit of a nightmare. Placing furniture larger than a side table turned into an extended game of trial and error, and storage space was pretty much nonexistent. So my job was simple: help turn the treehouse apartment of Adrian's childhood dreams into a functional, livable, grown-up home.

OPEN-DOOR POLICY

Adrian is the social activities director among her group of friends. Her apartment is where everyone meets before going out, and where they crash after. Unlike the other four units in this converted home, the attic had its own staircase along the side of the house that led straight to Adrian's front door—with a private porch to boot. (It was one of the reasons she chose this place—less chance of disturbing her neighbors.) The downside, however, was that the glass on these rounded doors—and the floor-level windows next to them—was completely clear when she moved in. So her "stop by whenever" policy led to a few too many post-shower surprise visitors.

Covering the windows with curtains was out of the question because of the windows' rounded shape. Plus, the landlord was adamant that we not touch any of the recently renovated walls or woodwork. So we found this decorative window film—which matched the existing architecture perfectly—at Home Depot for about $20 per sheet, and we cut the sheets to fit the windows. The film created a beautiful stained-glass effect in the entryway, while giving Adrian all the privacy she needed.

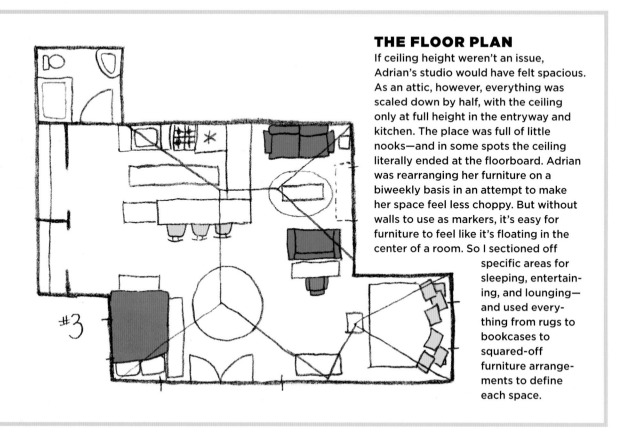

THE FLOOR PLAN

If ceiling height weren't an issue, Adrian's studio would have felt spacious. As an attic, however, everything was scaled down by half, with the ceiling only at full height in the entryway and kitchen. The place was full of little nooks—and in some spots the ceiling literally ended at the floorboard. Adrian was rearranging her furniture on a biweekly basis in an attempt to make her space feel less choppy. But without walls to use as markers, it's easy for furniture to feel like it's floating in the center of a room. So I sectioned off specific areas for sleeping, entertaining, and lounging—and used everything from rugs to bookcases to squared-off furniture arrangements to define each space.

THE MIX AND THE MATCH

Adrian's taste in décor was all over the charts. To put it simply, her philosophy was: "I know what I like when I see it." She had a clean-lined, midcentury modern sofa in marigold velvet, bright bohemian throw pillows, and a collection of vintage crochet afghans. We mixed in a yellow Victorian-style loveseat, a fuzzy sheepskin rug, graphic curtains, and a knotted fabric coffee table. In theory, none of these things "go" together. But that's what gave the space such great depth—and made it feel like Adrian.

PERFECTLY IMPERFECT SEATING

There was only one spot that had enough wall space to fit Adrian's midcentury modern sofa, and that was located right next to the kitchen. The sofa slid perfectly under the slanted ceiling, leaving just enough room for someone to sit comfortably without bumping his or her head. The problem became balance: without chairs or a coffee table to complete a fully rounded seating area, the sofa disappeared in the corner—making it a pretty uncompelling place to hang out.

We went in search of these missing pieces at the local antique warehouse, Paris on Ponce. Most cities have something similar: a giant strip of small antique dealers all under one roof. These places are great because vendors are far more likely to barter with you, since they're surrounded by competition. We picked up this Victorian-style loveseat and kidney-shape vanity—which we turned into a desk—for about $60. Back at Adrian's we placed the loveseat across from her sofa and finished off the space with a woven coffee table from Urban Outfitters and a small sheepskin rug picked up at Ikea. Then we dotted the place with plants (see page 213 for instructions on making your own vintage book planter) to make it feel even more like a true treehouse.

SEEING DOUBLE

There's nothing wrong with blending a number of styles in one space, but there should always be one repetitive element that makes everything seem a bit more cohesive. Here, that was the color yellow. You'll see various shades of it—from marigold to lemon—sprinkled around the living room.

TIP: In a room full of sharp angles, look for ways to introduce rounded elements, as we did with the kidney-shaped desk and circle-print curtains. It will keep your space from feeling too rigid.

OPPOSITE: I scattered small side tables around the apartment to make up for the fact that Adrian didn't have room for a proper dining table. When cleared off, they work as an impromptu place to eat.

WALL
STAMPS,
P. 221

VINTAGE BOOK
PLANTER, P. 213

HOW-TO: VINTAGE BOOK PLANTER

WHAT YOU NEED

- 1 leather bound book
- Elmer's Glue
- 1 small succulent
- Ruler
- Pen
- X-ACTO knife
- 1 quart-size Ziploc bag
- Scissors

STEP 1

Glue the pages of your book together by squiggling glue along the sides and gently pressing it into the pages with your fingers. Make sure not to glue the pages to the cover. Let dry completely, about 20 minutes.

STEP 2

Determine how wide of a space to cut for your succulent; you want at least 2 inches around the circumference of the roots to promote growth. Measure and trace the area you need to cut on the top page of your book.

STEP 3

Using your X-ACTO knife, carefully cut into the box you just drew. You will only be able to cut about 30 pages at a time, so you'll need to repeat this step until you've created a hole deep enough for your succulent.

STEP 4

Line the box you just cut with your plastic Ziploc bag, making sure the bottom and sides are covered.

STEP 5

Arrange your succulent on top of the Ziploc bag. Be sure to transfer enough soil from the original planter, along with the plant itself.

STEP 6

Using your scissors, trim the excess Ziploc bag around the edge of your succulent, leaving just enough of a plastic liner to keep water from running into the pages of the book when you water it.

THE SLEEPING NOOK

Bed placement is about so much more than where it happens to fit in a room. A good night's rest has to take priority over everything else. When Adrian first moved in, she tried placing her queen-size mattress on the ground in a small nook off the living area. It felt more private than anywhere else in the studio. But after a few nights of sleeping on the floor under low ceilings, things began to get a bit claustrophobic.

I wanted to give her a proper bed, and the only place to do that was in the small corner next to the front door. It had wide enough walls and high enough ceilings, but it meant covering two windows and coming up with a way to separate the mattress from the entryway. So I bought a tall bookcase from Ikea, painted it brown to match the existing woodwork, and slid the unit up against the bed. Being off the floor and having a skylight in the ceiling meant bouts of claustrophobia were no longer an issue. The bed ended up having a built-in, almost ship-like feel—and most importantly, Adrian felt completely relaxed in the space.

COUNT YOUR LUCKY STARS

Adrian's sleeping nook became her personal haven in an apartment laid out for company. It was where she watched movies on her computer, read the paper, or simply hung out and took advantage of that skylight. I wanted to make it as lounge-friendly as possible, so I lined the walls with extra-long pillows and gave her an ottoman at the foot of the bed. This opened up the possibilities of the space to so much more than just lying down. She could sit on the footstool and paint her nails, or prop herself up against the side wall with a book. When square footage is at a premium, the more functions you can use a particular area for, the happier you'll be.

Never hold back in small, segmented off areas: we selected a bedspread with a big, beautifully bold pattern and used it to punctuate the sleeping nook.

BOX IT UP

Once Adrian's sofa and bed were placed, all available wall space in the apartment was spoken for—leaving no room for a proper dresser (not that there was money left in the budget to buy one). So we decided to turn the bookcase into a giant chest of drawers, only instead of actual drawers she had twenty-five extra-deep boxes. This became a catchall for everything from clothes to bags to picnic supplies, since it was the only extensive storage in the entire apartment.

Originally, we'd discussed using baskets for this, but at ten dollars a piece that became an expensive project. These boxes from The Container Store cost a fraction of that, and after a couple coats of paint and the addition of some super-handy knobs they felt just as polished. It's easy for money-saving projects to turn into money-sucking projects instead—especially big ones—so make sure you start out with a budget and stick to it. For the amount of money we would have spent buying baskets, we could have gone out and found a whole new dresser.

WALL OF COLOR

Between the dark woodwork and the terracotta-colored walls, Adrian's apartment had a very masculine slant. And though her aesthetic was all over the place, "masculine" was the one thing it was not. Without the ability to paint the walls to combat this, I had to find more creative ways to add splashes of color in the apartment. By painting the visible sides of these boxes a bright purple, it introduced something distinctly feminine the second you walk in the door—effectively changing the mood of the whole apartment.

HOW-TO: PAINTED STORAGE BOXES

WHAT YOU NEED
- Storage box
- Semigloss paint
- Mini-paint roller
- Measuring tape
- Pencil
- Knob
- No. 10 washer (to coordinate with the knob screws)

STEP 1
Paint the visible sides of your storage box, and let dry completely—about 30 minutes.

STEP 2
Find and mark the center point on the front of your storage box.

STEP 3
Using the screw that came with your knob, gently poke it through your center mark. Pull the screw back out.

STEP 4
Slip a washer onto the end of your screw; then slide it back through the hole. (The washer is inside your box.) Screw on the top of your knob.

ARTS & CRAFTS CORNER

See those retro floral print pillows? Adrian made them, along with a lot of the other amazing throw pillows around the apartment. (She's a whiz with a set of crochet needles, too.) I really wanted to give her a place to spread out her craft projects, and make a huge mess if she wanted. So we turned the little nook that originally held her bed into an arts-and-crafts corner that doubled as a more laid-back place to hang out with friends. I threw down a plush shag rug, lined the wall with pillows, and gave her lots of baskets to hold crafting odds and ends. This became her favorite place to while away a lazy Sunday afternoon.

CIRCLE CIRCLE, DOT DOT

The wall may have been off-limits, but the landlord compromised by letting us paint a portion of the ceiling. This was our biggest opportunity to counteract all the sharp angles in the apartment, while also giving Adrian a wallpaper-like effect—which was something she really loved.

Now, if we had simply painted the ceiling a solid color, it would have emphasized the angles even more; but a graphic, repeating pattern actually opened up the space visually. So I made circle stamps out of a car wash sponge and invited a few of Adrian's friends over to help cover specific sections of her ceiling with painted dots (see page 221 for instructions on making your own wall stamps).

We focused our repeating dots on four portions of the ceiling that hung particularly low. And within those sections, we incorporated a larger diamond pattern by using circle stamps in two different colors—one dark, one light. This gave all those flat, blank walls tons of depth and personality.

If you're buying a rug that you plan on spending a decent amount of time sitting on, do yourself a favor and opt for a shaggy style—which tends to be softer because of all the extra pile. Trust me, your butt will thank you.

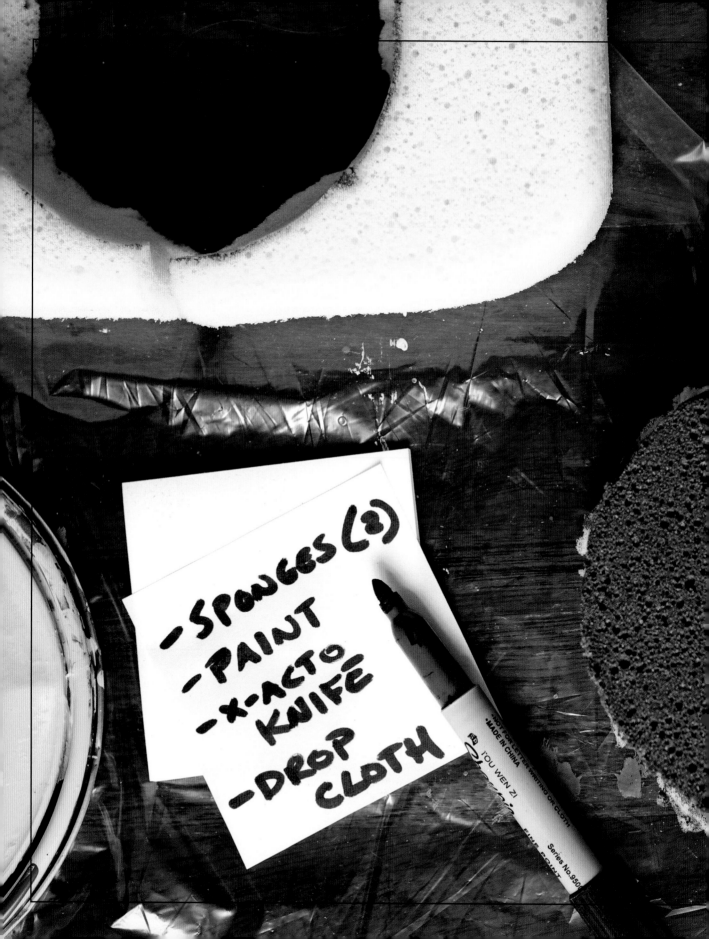

HOW-TO: WALL STAMPS

WHAT YOU NEED

- Sharpie
- Car wash sponge (one for each paint color)
- X-ACTO knife
- Drop cloth
- Paint (incorporate a second color for an extra pattern, if desired)

STEP 1

Trace your shape onto the sponge. Here, I used the top of a quart paint can as my guide for a circle—though technically, you can make almost any shape you want.

STEP 2

Using your X-ACTO knife carefully cut out your shape. Only the first inch of depth needs to have a clean edge, the rest can be a little ragged—since it won't be touching the wall.

STEP 3

Spread the drop cloth over your work area. Dip the top of the sponge into your paint, wiping off any excess on the side of your can. You don't want so much paint on your sponge that it causes drips on the wall.

STEP 4

Press—don't smash—the top of your sponge to the wall. If you're using a circle, rotate it clockwise. (This will get rid of any air pockets in your sponge.) Pull your sponge directly off the wall. Repeat as many times as you want!

Note: The goal here is not perfection; you want each stamp to be a little unique. You do not, however, want to end up with the old-school "sponging" effect. So once you press down your sponge, don't dab. This will ensure you get a clean, semi-texture-free stamp.

CHEAT SHEET:
THE BOHEMIAN

1
ENTERTAINING IS GREAT, but always make a private respite just for yourself—you'll need it.

2
STICK TO YOUR BUDGET when it comes to projects. It will often lead to a more creative solution.

3
BRING A BIT OF THE OUTSIDE IN: plants are the simplest way to make small spaces come alive.

4
BREAK UP SHARP ARCHITECTURAL ANGLES with a bold repeating pattern—as we did with the ceiling. It distracts the eye while visually overpowering all those harsh lines.

5
MAKING A BOHEMIAN AESTHETIC REALLY WORK requires a no-fear approach to mixing and matching. But add one recurring, unifying element (a color or material, for instance) to keep things from getting too wild.

BASEMENT
EMENTNASHVILLE.COM
THE COUPLE
E ALLEY ENTRANCE
1604

THE COUPLE

WHO: Tish & Ben

JOB: Musicians

LIVE IN: East Nashville

MEASUREMENTS:
1,000 square feet

TISH AND BEN THOUGHT THE TOUGHEST PART OF MOVING IN TOGETHER WAS DECIDING TO DO IT—THEN CAME MOVING DAY.

Tish showed up to their new loft, located in a refurbished turn-of-the-last-century cotton factory, with ten guitars and a set of keyboards. Ben brought his sound equipment and drum kits. The haul included all the makings of a band, but none of the bread-and-butter pieces you need for an apartment to be functional. Separately, the two had bounced between roommate-filled apartments and teeny-tiny studios, never investing in anything bigger than a mattress and box spring. So when they found this loft in East Nashville's warehouse district, the extra square footage was a luxury—it doubled as a practice space for their bands—but its emptiness was also intimidating.

One month of living in a sparse, echo-filled apartment and the two panicked. In an attempt to fill their loft, they took everything Tish's sister was giving up before moving cross-country—right down to a set of beat up bean bag chairs. Virtually overnight, their space went from too bare to too cluttered. That's the tricky thing about lofts—you've got to get the scale and the amount of furniture just right; otherwise the extra space turns into a curse. Tish and Ben needed help finding their own personalities in a space now full of hand-me-downs—a task made doubly tricky since this was the first merging of their things. Decorating became as much about figuring out what a marriage of their two styles should be as it was about what they wanted out of their apartment.

INSTRUMENTAL LIVING

TIP: To create coziness in a room with high ceilings, look for low-sitting furniture that will work in a close-knit arrangement.

PREVIOUS PAGE: Traveling gnomes are a building tradition. When any of Tish and Ben's neighbors have reason to celebrate, gnome statues "appear" in multiples at their front door.

Every musician comes with baggage (literally): the black cases that house their instruments are one big eyesore. When I arrived, all of Tish's guitars and all of Ben's drums were stashed at the back of the apartment. (I think they were hoping for an out-of-sight, out-of-mind scenario.) But this meant the picture window with its view of the Cumberland River was being wasted—as was the opportunity to inject music, something they both really love, into the décor.

By storing the cases and integrating the instruments throughout the loft, we freed up the corner by the window to make an intimate living room. We bought two loveseats, striped throw pillows, and a cowhide rug with our makeover money. I added two wicker chairs and a leather pouf they already owned for extra seating. Then I lined the wall with Tish's guitars and stacked Ben's drums in a corner, even turning one into a makeshift coffee table by topping it with a (removable) piece of precut glass. The space ended up having this graphic, rock-and-roll vibe.

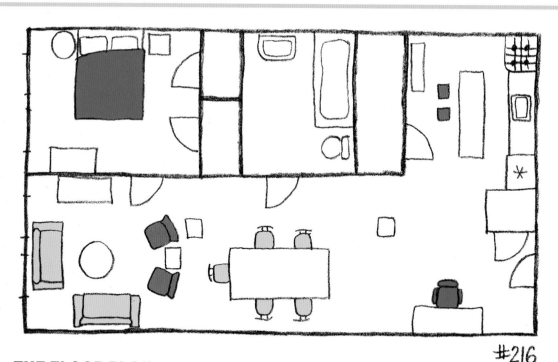

#216

THE FLOOR PLAN

This loft had wood plank floors, exposed-beam ceilings and large metal-frame windows—all beautiful architectural details, and all lost in the chaos of too much furniture. People think loft living means infinite amounts of room, when it can be more limiting than an apartment half its size. The reason: lack of room-defining walls. Creating distinct areas can be tricky to pull off. So the rule in cases like this should always be that less is more. We sold everything Tish and Ben didn't need. Then I divided the space— using the exposed wood beams as markers—into a living room and dining room. By breaking down one intimidatingly huge room into two manageably large areas, the loft felt fuller and more lived in.

READY. SET. ACTION.

One of the best pieces Tish and Ben inherited was this extra-long, traditional dining table that comfortably sat six. The downside, however, was that it didn't come with chairs, which posed a major blow to our budget. Tish and Ben wanted matching seating, which can be pretty expensive when you're looking for a set of six chairs. So we got creative and found these low-sitting director's chairs stacked in a corner at the local thrift store. We were able to haggle the price down to $240 for the whole lot. Use your imagination with seating, especially at a dining room table. Your only criteria should be finding something that fits under the table comfortably and is within your budget—after that, the more abstract, the better.

Having the space to host so many people is a luxury most twenty-somethings don't have, so I wanted to make this a fun spot to hang out. The dining room had two exposed beams, which acted as a border for the area. These markers gave me the option of making a really graphic (but contained) statement on the wall, so I painted big chevron stripes that raced all the way to the ceiling (see page 235 for instructions on painting your own chevron wall)—playing up the height and drawing attention to all the great, built-in woodwork. The finishing touch: an extra-large light fixture made from one box spring, two strands of globe lights, and some hanging hardware—inspired by something Tish had seen while on the road with her band (see page 233 for instructions on making your own box spring chandelier). All in all, this dramatic, expensive-looking dining area cost about $600.

"USE YOUR IMAGINATION WITH SEATING, ESPECIALLY AT A DINING ROOM TABLE. YOUR ONLY CRITERIA SHOULD BE FINDING SOMETHING THAT FITS UNDER THE TABLE COMFORTABLY AND IS WITHIN YOUR BUDGET."

BOX SPRING
CHANDELIER,
P. 233

CHEVRON
WALL,
P. 235

CHALK IT UP,
P. 233

CHALK IT UP

As previously discussed, my obsession with chalkboard paint knows no boundaries. I've never met a surface that wasn't far cooler after a couple of coats—and that includes furniture. Tish and Ben's table originally had a traditional cherry stain finish. I wanted to paint it black to match our director's chairs, and I decided at the last minute to use chalkboard paint instead. They now have this great interactive surface where they can sketch out a seating plan for dinner parties, play a game of beer pong, work on song lyrics, or simply let friends leave their parting wishes on the way out the door. The possibilities are as endless as the fun.

TIP: Fall in love with a particular doodle? Simply spray a coat of lacquer over the surface of your chalkboard paint and whatever's sketched on there will become a permanent fixture.

HOW-TO:
BOX SPRING CHANDELIER

WHAT YOU NEED

- Twin-size box spring
- Hammer
- 2 strands of globe lights
- Ladder (tall enough to reach the ceiling)
- 6 eye hooks
- 6 pieces of link chain (cut to the length your box spring should hang from the ceiling)
- 12 S hooks
- A willing set of helping hands
- Extra-long extension cord

STEP 1

Dismantle your box spring, so you're left with only the metal coil frame. All you need is a hammer (and some pent-up stress) to break the wooden border into smaller pieces that are relatively easy to tear off.

STEP 2

String your globe lights through your box spring, using the attached clips to connect each bulb to the metal frame. (For more light, you can always add another strand.)

STEP 3

Line up your box spring on the floor where you eventually want it to hang. Using your ladder, find the points on the ceiling that correspond with your box spring's four corners and the two halfway marks on both of its long sides. Screw your six eye hooks into the ceiling at these points.

STEP 4

Connect the link chain pieces to your box spring using six of your S hooks at the points that correspond with your eye hooks in the ceiling.

STEP 5

Grab a helper (or two), and hang your new box spring chandelier: connect the remaining S hooks to the opposite ends of your link chain pieces; then attach each one to an eye hook in the ceiling. (The box spring isn't heavy, just large and wobbly.)

STEP 6

Attach an extension cord to the end of your light strand. As discreetly as possible, run your cord up a chain, over the ceiling, and down a corner of the wall nearest to an electrical outlet. Plug in and enjoy!

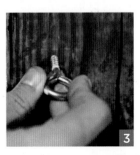

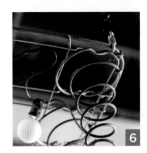

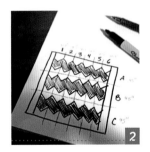
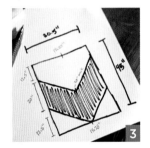

HOW-TO: CHEVRON WALL

WHAT YOU NEED

- Measuring tape
- 1 sheet of scrap paper
- Paint
- Paint roller
- Painter's tape
- Sharpie
- Pen

STEP 1
Measure the width and height of your wall.

STEP 2
Using scrap paper and these measurements, we'll figure out how to divide up the wall. (It's easier to sketch your measurements on paper first, before marking the wall.) I wanted 3 big stripes, so I divided the wall into 3 horizontal sections and 6 vertical sections. The number of vertical sections should be double the

horizontal to keep the zigzag ratio even.

STEP 3
Each of the 18 boxes you created by dividing your wall horizontally and vertically will contain its own V—since a chevron stripe is really just a series of V's. My stripe was 20 inches wide, so I centered that 20-inch measurement on both sides of my box, making a mark to designate the top and bottom of my stripe. Then I marked the middle point of the bottom line on my box, measured up 20 inches from there, and made another mark. Repeat these measurements in each of the 18 boxes.

STEP 4
Now that you have the measurements for your chevron stripe on paper, transfer those to the wall. Make a small

mark at the appropriate points, and play "connect the dots" with painter's tape.

STEP 5
Tape your V's up the wall first, and then move to the next vertical section. Be sure to tape sharp corners on the side of the tape that will be touching paint.

STEP 6
Apply at least 2 coats of paint to the appropriate sections. Let dry for 20 minutes.

STEP 7
Remove your tape and clean up any accidental drips. Let the paint dry for at least 2 hours before touching.

ISLAND TIME

Tish and Ben weren't the come-home-and-cook-every-night kinda couple. But they entertained often, which meant that when they put their culinary skills to use, it was for eight-plus people. Any host worth his or her weight in finger foods will tell you counter space is key to pulling off a meal this size—and there was little more than 3 feet of it in this loft. Come Friday night, they'd be stuck elbowing each other for room by the stove even though the alleyway kitchen was plenty big for the both of them. There was already an industrial hanging pot rack attached to a light fixture in the middle of the room, so I went out and found a restaurant supply table for about $200 to place underneath it. The table tripled the amount of counter space for food preparation, doubled as a drinks station for parties, and gave Tish and Ben a cozier spot to eat when it was just the two of them. If there's room for an island in your kitchen, take advantage—you'll love the extra surface area no matter how small.

TIP: To keep your stainless steel pieces nice and shiny, you have to invest in stainless steel cleaning wipes. Using multipurpose cleaners creates streaks and discolorations that become permanent after a while.

PAINTINGS BY NUMBER

Lots of little pieces of artwork were scattered among the loft's walls when I first arrived. There was a great collection of sentimental things that ranged from a portrait of Kurt Cobain to photos of Johnny Cash to pictures of Tish and Ben on stage with their own bands. The problem with this type of arrangement in large spaces is that small pieces end up getting glossed over. (I walked right by Tish's sketch of her dog without even noticing it.) The trick: grouping everything together in a gallery wall (see page 239 for instructions on organizing your own gallery wall). It draws focus to a single place; then lets the viewer take in each piece one at a time. You end up with the effect of a large-scale installation, but it's been puzzle-pieced together with the little things you love—which can (and should) include more than just framed photos and paintings.

THE (BREAKABLE) RULES OF WALL ARRANGING

- Place your biggest pieces first.
- Designate a top and bottom border, and stay within that area.
- Mix and match your sizes: if you have one big item, flank it with collections of smaller ones.

The kitchen lacked enough drawers to hold all of Tish and Ben's utensils, so I bought the straw boxes on the bottom shelf of the cart to store some of the larger items, like serving spoons and spatulas.

GALLERY

WALL

HOW-TO: GALLERY WALLS

WHAT YOU NEED

- 1 roll of 4-foot-wide craft paper
- Scissors
- Sharpie
- Painter's tape
- Picture hanging nails
- Hammer

STEP 1
Make a mock wall using your craft paper by rolling out the paper and cutting pieces to match the size of the space you want to fill on the wall—if necessary, you can tape 2 or 3 strips together.

STEP 2
Arrange the pieces you want to hang on the wall on your craft paper.

STEP 3
Once you have everything where you want it, take your Sharpie and carefully outline each piece on the craft paper. Then move everything to the side.

STEP 4
Tape your craft paper to the wall with painter's tape. Be precise about lining it up with the area you want to be your gallery wall.

STEP 5
At each outline, hammer a nail through the craft paper into the wall. Make sure to use the piece you plan to hang as a guide for where to place your nail, so it will hang straight.

STEP 6
Tear your craft paper off the wall, leaving all the nails intact. (Be sure you remember where everything goes.) Then hang all your pieces directly on the wall—they should line up perfectly.

HIS & HERS

TIP: Take baby steps into color, by trying small—cheaply replaced—items, like bright sheets in your bedroom. Every room needs a pop of color, but don't feel like you have to rush into something you may not love in the long run.

Tish likes vintage pieces with a lovingly worn finish, Ben likes things to be modern and streamlined. The bedroom is where these seemingly opposite aesthetics collided. This tends to be the hardest space for new couples to decorate because the bedroom has always been a personal retreat.

Between the two of them, Tish and Ben owned a set of side tables, a dresser, and a mattress/box spring set. They wanted the room to have a cozy, intimate feel, so we left the bed on the floor, where they could have unobstructed views of the sunrise every morning from the big metal-frame windows. Then, in an attempt to mix a little bit of Ben's style with a little bit of Tish's, I played bold patterns off solid details, like the traditional side tables and fuzzy throw pillows. There are elements of the rest of the apartment repeated in here, like the chevron stripe and rustic woodwork, but they take on their own softer identity that feels like the ideal blend of Tish and Ben.

GOING PLATINUM

Leaving the bed without a headboard felt far too "college days," so I wanted to add something to anchor the space and balance the high ceilings. I was scraping the bottom of the budget barrel, until Ben took me to one of his favorite record stores in Nashville. Out back I found McKay Used Books and CDs. They were selling vinyl in bulk at supercheap prices, so I bought almost ninety records for a grand total of $12.50—though you'll have a hard time finding anything you actually recognize (or want) in my haul. I came up with the idea of turning them into a makeshift headboard on the spot (see page 243 for instructions on making your own record headboard). What could be more perfect for two musicians? Anything can constitute a headboard—an old iron gate, a vintage slab of wood, even painted stripes on the wall. Let your imagination run wild.

Since the bedroom was separated from the main living area, I wanted to create a subtle sense of cohesiveness between the two spaces by repeating the chevron stripe from the wall on the bedspread—but in a totally new and unique way.

HOW-TO: RECORD HEADBOARD

WHAT YOU NEED

- Drop cloth
- Collection of records
- Matte charcoal, plastic-friendly spray paint
- 1.5-inch screws (as many as you have records)
- Electric drill

STEP 1

Spread the records out on top of the drop cloth. If you want to leave the records "as is" with the titles and vinyl unpainted, skip the rest of Steps 1 and 2. Otherwise, start spray-painting the top of your records, keeping the nozzle of the can 10 to 12 inches away from the surface. Let dry for 20 minutes.

STEP 2

Apply a second coat of spray paint, making sure to even out any streaks or drips. Let dry for another 20 minutes.

STEP 3

Starting along the floorboard, attach each record to the wall by drilling a screw through its center hole. Work your way across the bottom until you have the desired width of your "headboard."

STEP 4

Using your bottom row as a guide, work your way up the wall, stacking each new record directly on top of the one below, so that the edges just barely touch. Stop with your last full record, before reaching the ceiling.

CHEAT SHEET:
THE COUPLE

1

LOFT SPACES CAN BE INTIMIDATING; start by defining specific areas, and then add furniture.

2

DON'T TRY TO FIT A CIRCLE INTO A SQUARE PEG. If something you own doesn't work in your new space, sell it and use the money to buy something that does.

3

CREATE A GALLERY WALL WITH A GROUP OF ARTWORKS. It's an interesting (and easy) way for lots of little pieces to make one big impact.

4

WHEN DEALING WITH HIGH CEILINGS and open floor plans, rely on low-sitting furniture to create a sense of intimacy.

5

GREAT ARCHITECTURAL DETAILS ARE like an interior design freebie— so make sure you're taking advantage.

THE RESOURCE GUIDE

RESOURCES BY CHAPTER

You saw it in the book.
You have to have it.
Well, here's where to
find it.

THE ART LOVER
IN NYC

PAINT
benjaminmoore.com

Benjamin Moore
San Antonio Gray
- Main room walls

Benjamin Moore
Twilight Zone
- Bathroom stripes,
  doors, fireplace mantle

Benjamin Moore
Bright Yellow
- Busts, desk,
  kitchen frame

Benjamin Moore
Chalkboard
- Kitchen wall

**STORES AND
FLEA MARKETS**

Hell's Kitchen
Flea Market
West 39th St., between
Ninth and Tenth Aves.
- Desk chair, frames,
  kitchen jars
  hellskitchenflea
  market.com

Goodwill
44 West 8th St.
- Desk
  goodwill.org

Mood Fabrics
225 West 37th St., 3rd Fl.
- Pillow fabric, oilcloth
  moodfabrics.com

CB2
451 Broadway
- Throw pillow on bed
  cb2.com

West Elm
112 West 18th St.
- Shower curtain
  westelm.com

ONLINE RETAILERS

FLOR
- Carpet tiles
  flor.com

Blik
- Dot wall decals
  whatisblik.com

Plaster Craft
- Busts
  plastercraft.com

Overstock
- Barstools
  overstock.com

Target
- Throw pillows on sofa
  target.com

Pier 1 Imports
- Desk lamp
  pier1.com

THE FREE SPIRIT
IN SAN FRANCISCO

PAINT
benjaminmoore.com

Benjamin Moore
Coral Spice
- Living room

Benjamin Moore
November Skies
- Kitchen

**STORES AND
FLEA MARKETS**

Lotus Bleu
325 Hayes St.
- Dining room curtains
  lotusbleudesign.com

CB2
34 Ellis St.
- Coffee table, rug,
  hanging vases,
  dining table
  cb2.com

Past Perfect
2224 Union St.
- Reading chair
  pastperfectsf.com

Funky Furniture
1100 Folsom St.
- Sofa, throw pillow,
  desk chair
  funkyfurnituresf.com

Moving Sale
952 Howard St.
- Dining chairs
  movingsale.biz

Pier 1 Imports
555 9th St.
- Bed throw pillow
  pier1.com

ONLINE RETAILERS

World Market
- Pouf
  worldmarket.com

Live Well Designs
- Lampshade, kitchen
  magnet board
  livewelldesigns.com

Tempaper
- Temporary wallpaper
  tempaperdesigns.com

Amazon
- Headboard
  amazon.com

Mondial Lus
- Thumbtacks
  sweetbellausa.com

THE PREPPY
IN CLEVELAND

PAINT
benjaminmoore.com

Benjamin Moore
Soft Jazz
- Living room walls

Benjamin Moore
Sterling Silver
- Bedroom walls,
  kitchen frame

Benjamin Moore
Huntington Green
- Argyle wall

Benjamin Moore
Amherst Gray
- Argyle wall

Benjamin Moore
Oxford White
- Dining chair stripe

STORES AND
FLEA MARKETS

Bed Bath & Beyond
4031 Richmond Rd.,
Warrensville Heights
- Round glass table tops
  bedbathandbeyond
  .com

Jo-Ann Fabric and Craft
2203 Warrensville Center
Rd., University Heights
- Ribbon banding
  joann.com

Flower Child
11508 Clifton Blvd.
- Lamps
  flowerchildvintage.com

Target
14070 Cedar Rd.,
University Heights
- Dining chairs
  target.com

Unique Thrift Store
3333 Lorain Ave.
- Bedroom pillows, lamps
  uniquethriftstore.com

Thriftique/NCJW
26055 Emery Rd., Unit C,
Warrensville Heights
- Trunk
  ncjwcleveland.org

ONLINE RETAILERS

CB2
- Acrylic easel
  cb2.com

Dash & Albert
- Living room and
  bedroom area rugs
  dashandalbert.com

Grandin Road
- Coffee table cubes
  grandinroad.com

Mortise & Tenon
- Sofa
  mortisetenon.com

Payless Decor
- Woven shades
  paylessdecor.com

Canvas on Demand
- Blueberry print transfer
  canvasondemand.com

Treasurbite Studio
- Bedroom image
  joeschmelzer.com

I Am Human Now
- Laptop cover
  iamhumannow.com

THE ROOMMATES
IN BOSTON

PAINT
benjaminmoore.com

Benjamin Moore
Elephant Gray
- Living room side table

Benjamin Moore
Majestic Blue
- Dining chair

Benjamin Moore
Old Claret
- Dining chair

Benjamin Moore
Raspberry Blush
- Dining bench

STORES AND
FLEA MARKETS
Grey's Fabric & Notions
450 Harrison Ave., #63
- Curtain and panel
  fabric
  greysfabric.com

Cambridge
Antique Market
201 Msgr. O'Brien
Highway, Cambridge
- Dining chairs
  marketantique.com

West Elm
160 Brookline Ave.
- Anne's bedding
  westelm.com

Bed Bath & Beyond
401 Park Dr.
- Shower curtain,
  pink throw pillow
  bedbathandbeyond
  .com

Anthropologie
799 Boylston St.
- Dresser knobs
  anthropologie.com

Urban Outfitters
361 Newbury St.
- Wall flowers
  urbanoutfitters.com

Winmil Fabrics
111 Chauncy St.
- Canvas headboard
  fabric
  617-542-1815

ONLINE RETAILERS
FLOR
- Carpet tiles
  flor.com

Blik
- Headboard wall decals
  whatisblik.com

THE COLLECTOR
IN LA

STORES AND
FLEA MARKETS
Cleveland Art
110 North Santa Fe Ave.
- Coffee table
  clevelandart.com

Croft House
326 North La Brea Ave.
- Bookcase
  crofthouse.com

Michael Levine
920 Maple Ave.
- Camo pillow
  mlfabric.com

Amsterdam Modern
4011 West Sunset Blvd.
- Ottoman
  amsterdammodern.com

The Framing
House Design
942 North Broadway
- Target frame
  213-621-0295

Urban Home
15301 Ventura Blvd.,
Sherman Oaks
- Dining table
  shopurbanhome.com

Urban Outfitters
330 North San Fernando
Blvd., Burbank
- Lamps
  urbanoutfitters.com

CB2
8000 West Sunset Blvd.
- Bed throw pillows
  cb2.com

ONLINE RETAILERS
Pottery Barn
- Doormat
  potterybarn.com

FLOR
- Bedroom carpet tiles
  flor.com

Room & Board
- Blanket
  roomandboard.com

THE SCHOLAR
IN CHICAGO

PAINT
benjaminmoore.com

Benjamin Moore
American Cheese
- Living room slats
  and stencil

Benjamin Moore
Southfield Green
- Bedroom wall

STORES AND
FLEA MARKETS
Crate and Barrel Outlet
1864 North Clybourn Ave.
- Living room throw
  pillows
  crateandbarrel.com

FLOR
1873 North Clybourn
- Carpet tiles
  flor.com

West Elm
1000 West North Ave.
- Papier maché bust,
  bedding, kitchen
  curtain
  westelm.com

Praha
3849 North Lincoln Ave.
- Map, nightstand
  773-549-1227

Home Depot
2570 North Elston Ave.
- Kitchen knobs
  homedepot.com

ONLINE RETAILERS
Stencil 1
- Living room stencils
  stencil1.com

World Market
- Bedroom lamp,
  counter stools
  worldmarket.com

Wallies
- Chalkboard decals
  wallies.com

Blik
- Mirror frame decals
  whatisblik.com

THE REBEL
IN SEATTLE

PAINT
benjaminmoore.com

Benjamin Moore
Sea Reflections
- Faded wall treatment

Benjamin Moore
Topaz
- Kitchen and bathroom
  walls, doorway
  bookcase

STORES AND
FLEA MARKETS
IKEA
601 SW 41st St., Renton
- White curtains,
  coffee tables
  ikea.com

Home Depot
2701 Utah Ave. South
- Pipe curtain rod
  homedepot.com

Target
302 NE Northgate Way
- Lamp, fan
  target.com

Goodwill
1765 6th Ave. South
- Throw pillow,
  mailbox, lamp
  goodwill.org

Urban Outfitters
401 Broadway East
- Wall clock, area rug
  urbanoutfitters.com

Value Village
1525 11th Ave.
- Kitchen jars and bowls
  valuevillage.com

ONLINE RETAILERS
Bemz
- Sofa slipcover
  bemz.com

Live Well Designs
- Lampshade
  livewelldesigns.com

Re-Surface
- Graffiti lamp
  on bookcase
  re-surface.net

Skurniture
- Skateboard table
  skurniture.com

Treasurbite Studio
- Photograph
  joeschmelzer.com

2Jane
- Tile tattoos
  2jane.com

THE HOMEBODY
IN LA

PAINT
benjaminmoore.com

Benjamin Moore
Waynesboro Taupe
- Living room, bedroom, kitchen walls

Benjamin Moore
Morning Coffee
- Bedroom circle

STORES AND
FLEA MARKETS
Urban Home
15301 Ventura Blvd.,
Sherman Oaks
- Coffee table
  shopurbanhome.com

Amsterdam Modern
4011 West Sunset Blvd.
- Ottoman
  amsterdammodern.com

The Container Store
10250 Santa Monica
Blvd.
- Wood boxes
  containerstore.com

**Ta Fong Restaurant
Supply**
121 West Elmyra St.
- Kitchen shelves
  tafongusa.com

Pier 1 Imports
5711 Hollywood Blvd.
- Kitchen canisters
  pier1.com

Pepe's Thrift Shop
2504 West Sunset Blvd.
- Bed
  213-483-1049

Target
7100 Santa Monica Blvd.
- Lamp
  target.com

Michael Levine
920 Maple Ave.
- Cowhide rug
  mlfabric.com

The Sofa Company
100 West Green St.,
Pasadena
- Sofa
  thesofaco.com

ONLINE RETAILERS
Ballard Designs
- Living room floor lamp
  ballarddesigns.com

Napa Style
- Area rug
  napastyle.com

Etsy
- British flag pillow
  etsy.com

Graham & Brown
- Wallpaper
  grahambrown.com

Payless Decor
- Window blinds
  paylessdecor.com

The Animal Print Shop
- Owl print
  theanimalprintshop.com

Craigslist
- Desk
  losangeles.craigslist.org

Serena & Lily
- Bedding
  serenaandlily.com

Cardboard Safari
- Cardboard deer head
  cardboardsafari.com

THE BOHEMIAN
IN ATLANTA

PAINT
benjaminmoore.com

Benjamin Moore
Plum Perfect
- Storage boxes

Benjamin Moore
Oakwood Manor
- Stamp wall

Benjamin Moore
Abbey Brown
- Stamp wall, bookcase

STORES AND
FLEA MARKETS
Paris on Ponce
716 Ponce de Leon
Place NE
- Desk, chair
  parisonponce.com

Home Depot
650 Ponce de Leon
- Window film
  homedepot.com

Urban Outfitters
1061 Ponce de Leon
Ave. NE
- Coffee table, bedding
  urbanoutfitters.com

IKEA
441 16th St. NW
- Curtain and purple rug
  ikea.com

Pier 1 Imports
3435 Lenox Rd. NE
- Throw pillows
  pier1.com

The Container Store
3255 Peachtree Rd. NE
- Storage boxes
  containerstore.com

West Elm
260 18th St. NW
- Throw pillows
  westelm.com

ONLINE RETAILERS
Flokati
- Shaggy rug
  flokatirug.net

THE COUPLE
IN NASHVILLE

PAINT
benjaminmoore.com

Benjamin Moore
Emerald Isle
- Chevron stripe

Benjamin Moore
Pigeon Gray
- Kitchen wall

Benjamin Moore
Chalkboard
- Dining room table

STORES AND
FLEA MARKETS
Gaslamp Antiques
100 Powell Place,
Ste. 200
- Cowhide, dining chairs
  gaslampantiques.com

Unique Thrift Store
4802 Charlotte Pike
- Box spring
  uniquethriftstore.com

West Elm
4019 Hillsboro Pike
- Duvet, reading lamp
  westelm.com

**McKay Used Books &
CDs**
5708 Charlotte Pike
- Records
  mckaybooks.com

Target
26 White Bridge Rd.
- Sheets
  target.com

ONLINE RETAILERS
**Advanced Modern
Interiors**
- Sofas
  advancedinterior
  design.com

Redefine Home
- Striped pillows
  redefinehome.com

Dash & Albert
- Area rug
  dashandalbert.com

Working Class Studio
- Throw pillow
  workingclassstudio.com

RESOURCES BY SUBJECT

Shop like a pro with our little black book of the best stores and websites around.

ON THE WALL

WALLPAPER, WALL DECALS, AND STENCILS

2Modern
2modern.com
- Wall decals and canvas art

2 Jane
2jane.com
- Tile tattoos

Blik
whatisblik.com
- Wall decals

Couture Déco
couturedeco.com
- Decals and temporary wallpaper

Cutting Edge Stencils
cuttingedgestencils.com
- Large wall stencils

Design Your Wall
designyourwall.com
- Custom removable wallpaper and decals

Ferm Living
fermlivingshop.com
- Innovative wall decals

Graham & Brown
grahambrown.com
- Wallpaper, including removable options

Stencil 1
stencil1.com
- Wall stencils

ART

20x200
20x200.com
- Limited-edition art and photography prints

The Animal Print Shop
theanimalprintshop.com
- Limited-edition animal photography prints

Art.com
- Largest online archive of affordable art prints

Art Muse
artmuse.com
- Contemporary art prints, searchable by price

Canvas On Demand
canvasondemand.com
- Custom canvas photo wraps

The Condé Nast Store
condenaststore.com
- Archival prints from all their publications

La-La Land Posters
lalalandposters.com
- Retro poster reprints

Penny Lane
pennylanepublishing.com
- Affordable selection of large canvas art prints

Pop Chart Lab
popchartlab.com
- Graphic chart posters

Society6
society6.com
- Limited-edition prints from contemporary artists around the world

The Working Proof
theworkingproof.com
- Limited-edition art prints with a charitable twist

Z Gallerie
zgallerie.com
- Affordable selection of large-scale art prints

Zatista
zatista.com
- Original artwork, searchable by price

OTHER

Cardboard Safari
cardboardsafari.com
- Eco-friendly cardboard trophy heads

LG Custom Accessories
lgcustomaccessories.com
- Custom bulletin boards

FURNITURE

Advanced Interior Designs
advancedinterior designs.com
- Affordable selection of furniture

American Furnishings
americanfurnishings.com
- Reasonably priced industrial chairs and bar stools

Amsterdam Modern
amsterdammodern.com
- Vintage Danish furniture

Apt 2B
apt2b.com
- Affordable selection of modern furniture

Ballard Designs
ballarddesigns.com
- Traditional furniture; good periodic sales

BoConcept
boconcept.com
- Modern accessories

Brocade Home
brocadehome.com
- Feminine furniture and accessories

CB2
cb2.com
- Modern furniture, tabletop, and accessories with a loft-like aesthetic

Chiasso
chiasso.com
- Affordable selection of contemporary furniture and accessories

Croft House
crofthouse.com
- Reasonably priced reclaimed industrial wood furniture

EQ3
eq3.com
- Affordable selection of contemporary furniture

Evinco Design
evincodesign.com
- Great clearance section with designer modern furniture

Gaiam
gaiam.com
- Eco-friendly furniture and accessories

Grandin Road
grandinroad.com
- Affordable selection of furniture—and great holiday décor

Grounded
shopgrounded.com
- Mid-range furniture, rugs, tabletop, and accessories

Hayneedle
hayneedle.com
- Traditional furniture

Home Decorators
homedecorators.com
- Traditional furniture

Industry West
industry-west.com
- Affordable selection of industrial furniture

Lushpad
lushpad.com
- Buy/sell marketplace for modern furniture

Napa Style
napastyle.com
- Rustic furniture with a good clearance section

Room & Board
roomandboard.com
- Great clearance section with modern furniture

Serena & Lily
serenaandlily.com
- Traditional furniture and accessories with a great bazaar section and sales

Urban Outfitters
urbanoutfitters.com
- On-trend side tables, headboards, and wall décor

Viva Terra
vivaterra.com
- Eco-friendly furniture and accessories

Wayfair
wayfair.com
- Excellent furniture selection and prices; great "quick ship" section for last-minute needs

Wisteria
wisteria.com
- Traditional furniture with a great clearance section

World Market
worldmarket.com
- Global-styled affordable furniture, accessories, and specialty food

ON THE FLOOR

Dash & Albert
dashandalbert.com
- Affordable timeless rugs

FLOR
flor.com
- One of the best resources for floor coverings

Morris Etc.
morrisetc.com
- Vibrant floor coverings

Overstock
overstock.com
- Great resource for low-priced rugs

The Perfect Rug
theperfectrug.com
- Custom affordable rugs

ALL THE EXTRAS

2Modern
2modern.com
- Look for sales on their great (but pricey) pillows

Alice Supply Co.
alicesupplyco.com
- Trendy housewares and tools

Angela Adams
angelaadams.com
- Modern tabletop accessories

Bemz
bemz.com
- Slipcovers for IKEA sofas and chairs

Burke Decor
burkedecor.com
- Great assortment of tabletop and accessories

Calico Corners
calicocorners.com
- Fabrics sold by the yard and free swatches

The Company Store
thecompanystore.com
- Affordable bedding and bath

The Container Store
containerstore.com
- All your storage essentials

Crate & Barrel
crateandbarrel.com
- Glassware, throw pillows, and accessories

Emmo Home
emmohome.com
- Modern tabletop and accessories

Etsy
etsy.com
- Handmade treasures

IKEA
ikea.com
- Curtains, fabric selection, accessories, rugs, and mix-and-match tables

Lamps Plus
lampsplus.com
- All things lighting related

Mirror Mate
mirrormate.com
- Affordable custom frames for your bathroom mirror

ModCloth
modcloth.com
- Quirky vintage accessories

Nettleton Hollow
nettletonhollow.com
- Dried florals that will last a lifetime

Olde Good Things
ogtstore.com
- Architectural salvage

Payless Decor
paylessdecor.com
- Affordable selection of custom window blinds and roman shades

Pendleton
pendleton-usa.com
- Americana blankets and pillows

Pier 1 Imports
pier1imports.com
- Vibrant pillows, accent chairs, and accessories

Plaster Craft
plastercraft.com
- Statues and busts

Pottery Barn
potterybarn.com
- Great prices on rugs and frequent sales

PBTeen
pbteen.com
- Funky furniture and accessories, not just for teens

Pylones
pylones-usa.com
- Quirky tabletop and kitchen accessories

Re-Surface
re-surface.net
- Graffiti-inspired lighting

Saffron Marigold
saffronmarigold.com
- Indian-inspired linens

Shades of Light
shadesoflight.com
- Lighting and rugs

Skurniture
skurniture.com
- Skateboard furniture

West Elm
westelm.com
- Great selection of curtains and bedding

Working Class Studio
workingclassstudio.com
- Products designed by the students of SCAD

FLASH SALE SITES

The Foundary
shop.thefoundary.com
- Great deals on a wide array of furniture

Gilt Home
gilt.com
- Upscale vendors at a fraction of the normal cost

HauteLook
hautelook.com
- Curated, always hip sales featuring an ever-changing inventory

One Kings Lane
onekingslane.com
- Reduced high-end furniture, rugs, and accessories

PRICE CHECK

Amazon
amazon.com
- Great place to search for better prices on items

eBay
ebay.com
- Before buying anything "faux" vintage. Check eBay for the real thing. It's often there and priced better than the knockoff

ShopStyle
shopstyle.com
- Invaluable resource that compares different websites and prices for furniture searches you input

HEY, YOU. YOU'RE AWESOME.

This book would not have been possible without the support of my family and all the families involved. To my partner in crime, Joe Schmelzer, I will be forever grateful to you for creating these spaces with me and then turning them into inspiring photographs to share. I truly could not have done this book without you. Heather Summerville morphed my scattered ideas into a beautifully written book for you all to enjoy. Her tireless efforts at perfecting every word and sentence are what make this book special. I want to thank Betsy Amster for turning our idea into a reality, Rae Ann Spitzenberger for laying this book out so stylishly, and Aliza Fogelson for believing in this project from the beginning. A big shout-out is in order to the team at Benjamin Moore for letting us showcase their beautiful colors and quality product; I cannot sing their praises enough. Last but not least, thanks to all the people who opened their homes to me for this project. I loved transforming your spaces, but more important, I loved sharing your stories.

INDEX